THE ALL-TIME
BIGGEST
SPORTS JERKS

And Other Goofballs, Cads,
Miscreants, Reprobates, and
Weirdos (Plus a Few Good Guys)

Michael Freeman

TRIUMPH
BOOKS

This book is available in quantity at special discounts for your group or organization. For further information, contact:

Triumph Books
542 South Dearborn Street
Suite 750
Chicago, Illinois 60605
(312) 939–3330
Fax (312) 663–3557

Printed in U.S.A.
ISBN: 978-1-60078-178-0
Design by Sue Knopf
Photos courtesy of AP Images unless otherwise indicated.

"…I am not a bum. I'm a jerk. I once had wealth, power, and the love of a beautiful woman. Now I only have two things: my friends and…uh… my Thermos."

—Steve Martin in *The Jerk*

Contents

*Presented in **alphabetical order** because I'm not giving the rankings away that easily, here are the* All-Time Biggest Sports Jerks:

vi

Introduction

We begin with noted thespian and wordsmith Mike Tyson, who earns a highly respectable No. 25 position on the all-time greatest sports jerks list because he has produced some of the most bizarre, frightening, and mind-boggling moments ever—not to mention some of the more delicious quotes in sports history.

"My power is discombobulatingly devastating," Tyson once said. "I could feel his muscle tissues collapse under my force. It's ludicrous these mortals even attempt to enter my realm."

And: "I guess I'm gonna fade into Bolivian."

And: "I can sell out Madison Square Garden masturbating."

This gem was produced by Mr. Tyson during a press conference with reporters, "I'm on the Zoloft to keep from killing y'all."

And perhaps one of the top 10 sports quotations ever delivered, "Lennox Lewis, I'm coming for you, man. My style is impetuous. My defense is impregnable, and I'm just ferocious. I want your heart. I want to eat his children. Praise be to Allah!"

Not exactly "Four score and seven years ago," but Tyson does make his point.

Convicted rapist, ear biter, deadbeat, sociopath, drug user, perennial hoosegow resident...other than that, the perfect gentleman. And Tyson doesn't even crack the top 20 on the jerk list. Imagine that.

This is the book of the sordid, the corrupt, the morbid, and the psycho. A la-la land where Bobby Knight is legend, Barry Bonds is the president, Ron Artest is the vice admiral of fan relations, Michael Vick heads animal control, Robert Irsay is the minister of finance, Tim Donaghy is head of the gambling prevention department, Bill Belichick is the secretary of defense, and Ty Cobb is the secretary of state.

There are steroids in baseball, crooked game officials in basketball, and the salaciousness of Peeping Toms with video cameras in the shenanigan known as Spygate. If there was ever a time for the chronicling of needle-pinched jerks in all of their glorious jerkiness, the time is now.

For some of these jerks, you don't get your popcorn ready; you get your penicillin ready.

To the gamblers, degenerates, sexual harassers, cheap-shot artists, performance enhancers, perverts, dog fighters, girlfriend stealers, egoists, nudists, thugs, videographers, spit connoisseurs, stripper lovers, and too-sexy-for-your-bad-selves pretty boys, we salute you, jerks all.

You, too, John Daly.

This book, most of all, is meant to be in jest, poking fun at the men and women on playing fields across the sports spectrum currently involved in their extended adolescence and baby-mama making. We also salute the good guys in sports (though it seems there are fewer and fewer left).

There was the opportunity for me to pen the sequel to *War and Peace*, but I selected this jerk masterpiece instead. Please feel free to call me a jerk for naming these jerks because, after all, it takes a jerk to know 100 jerks. Or does it take 100 jerks to know one jerk? My jerk trigonometry is suddenly all discombobulatingly nondevastating.

The All-Time Biggest Sports Jerks is based on the series written by the author for CBSSports.com. But this book is remarkably better. Well, a little better. Well, a tiny bit better. Well...never mind.

Deciding on the order of the list was painstaking, and only the most brilliant scientists, engineers, astronauts, and chemists were consulted—as was Terry Bradshaw. The secret formula that determined the list is locked away in Nate Newton's tummy and was compiled in an undisclosed location with my jerk genius fueled solely by lemonade and nandrolone. So, as former Arizona and Minnesota coach Dennis Green might say, "If you want to crown my ass, then crown me."

Yet make no mistake—there is a serious point to this book. It is...damn, what was the point again?

Hall of Fame linebacker Lawrence Taylor was once asked what he could do better than any other linebacker in history.

His reply: "Drink."

The All-Time Biggest Sports Jerks toasts to that.

Tiki Barber

"We got outcoached."

—TIKI BARBER IN 2006,
RIPPING NEW YORK GIANTS COACH
TOM COUGHLIN

"That's football. It's not complicated. This is something that teams and kids and coaches do from 12-years-old to college and beyond. It isn't rocket science."

—BARBER RIPPING COUGHLIN AGAIN
OVER NOT RUNNING THE BALL ENOUGH

"I don't know if he realizes how much $17 million is. That is absolutely ridiculous, to turn that down. He's already the highest-paid defensive player in the league. He's already making more than most quarterbacks....Michael is not thinking about the team; he's thinking about himself."

—BARBER RIPPING TEAMMATE MICHAEL STRAHAN
FOR A CONTRACT DISPUTE IN 2002

Have you ever met someone who believed they were the smartest person in the room and wanted everyone to know it? Do you know someone who relishes pointing out what others are doing incorrectly but refuses to look in the mirror? We all know someone like that (and stop pointing at me). There is no better living embodiment of this than Atiim Kiambu Hakeem-ah otherwise known as Tiki Barber.

Jerkdom is difficult to define. It's similar to the Supreme Court justice who once stated he wasn't exactly certain what pornography was but knew it when he saw it. Jerkdom isn't pornography (which is too bad), but jerkdom is an ethereal state of jerkiness. You just know it. Jerkiness taps you on the shoulder and says "hello" before giving you a wedgie. In many ways, Barber defines jerkdom.

Just before the 2008 season, several New York Giants players were discussing their old teammate Barber and a bizarre controversy to which he'd found himself glued. The controversy began when Barber was discussing the Olympics and medal counts with a woman co-host on MSNBC when it appeared Barber used an offensive word referring to the female anatomy. The phrase Barber appeared to use was "gold medal cunt." As in the anchor was a "gold medal cunt." Barber was irritated that the woman mocked him for not having a Super Bowl ring. Barber denied using the word, but if you had ears, it was easy to determine he did.

Some Giants players got a huge kick out of the controversy, according to one person close to the players. Let's just say there were some in the Giants locker room not exactly sad to see Barber stuck in his predicament. Apparently Giants fans also remember how Barber treated some of his teammates and coaches during his New York playing career. During New York's preseason game against Cleveland at Giants Stadium in 2008, footage of Barber was shown on the scoreboard and was met with a raucous round of boos.

When Barber was a Giant, he basically called Strahan greedy, Coughlin a grumpy old goat that took the joy out of football, and Manning a gold-medal runt. How times have changed. Coughlin has a ring, and Barber doesn't. Strahan has a ring, and Barber doesn't.

Media Non-Jerks

Barber's now in the media, meaning by nature he's jerk material. Yet not all media types are jerks (why must you continue pointing at me?). Here are five sports media non-jerks. They're sports media good guys if you can believe such a thing exists.

5. **Dan Patrick** – He might have the best sports talk radio show in the business and is actually one of the more laid-back stars in sports journalism.

4. **Jemele Hill** – The only thing tougher than being an opinionated African American sports journalist is being a female African American sports journalist. She's not perfect, but Hill handles the criticism well and possesses serious ability.

3. **Jay Glazer** – Currently the best pure reporter in all of sports journalism, yet Glazer hasn't allowed his skyrocketing success to affect his bald head. Glazer breaks more stories than anyone in the business.

2. **Stephen A. Smith** – Yells a lot. Then he yells some more. Then after that, he might yell again. He is also one of the most laid-back and friendly people you will ever meet. He's also good.

1. **Andrea Kremer** – The most well-rounded of all sports journalists, Kremer can work an Olympics, NFL game or cause a hardened interview subject to cry with pertinent questions. She's also a dedicated mom.

Strahan possesses a television career that could end up better than Barber's. Manning has a ring and, well, you get the point.

Barber was a catalyst, almost a leader, of the anti-Coughlin mob several years ago. He wanted Coughlin gone and played to a New York media that whined about Coughlin because he made their jobs more difficult. Upon retiring, Barber stuck his pitchfork further into Coughlin's lower back by saying Coughlin was a big reason he left football. What Barber did to Manning was in many ways even worse. By publicly embarrassing Manning and portraying him as a clueless-goober trust-fund baby incapable of leading men—an incomparable sin for an NFL quarterback— Barber was purposely trying to undermine Manning. Since then, Manning has undergone one of the more stunning transformations we've ever witnessed in an NFL quarterback. Manning didn't just prove Barber wrong. He proved probably millions wrong and might likely continue to do so. It's entirely possible Manning will end up winning another Super Bowl within a few years.

There is nothing more gratifying than watching a player so many people (including an occasionally smarmy ex-running back named Atiim Kiambu Hakeem-ah) thought would fall on his pedigreed butt succeed in a major way. What if Eli ends up winning more titles than his brother, Peyton? It's definitely possible. The younger Manning has come a long way since some awkward-looking photographs of him appeared on the Internet several years ago. In one, Manning looked blitzed, not by a linebacker, but by a number of tall cold ones. His eyes were barely open and he resembled a co-star from *Dude, Where's My Car?*

Now Manning's starring in *Tiki, Here's My Ring. Where's yours?*

 # Jose Canseco

In physics, there are matter and anti-matter. In jerks, there are jerks and anti-jerks. Unfortunately, the anti-jerks are an endangered species, but one decided to rise up and take a strong stand against the spreading disease of jerkdom. His name is Vai Sikahema, and he did something many people would love to do. He bashed in the face of Jose Canseco.

This should make Sikahema eligible for the Congressional Medal of Honor, but the Jedi Jerk Council offers him something better: the Anti-Jerk Medal of Honor. Which would you rather have?

This is the moment that shook up the jerk universe. Canseco and Sikahema met in a celebrity boxing match in Atlantic City, New Jersey, in the summer of 2008. Canseco is 6'4" and 250 pounds. Sikahema is seven inches shorter and 40 pounds lighter. Canseco should have stomped out Sikahema's guts. But something strange happened. The much smaller Sikahema just flat-out intimidated Canseco from the very beginning. When they met at center ring, Sikahema was literally looking up Canseco's nose. He was that much shorter. That didn't prevent Sikahema from stating, "I'm going to knock you down."

Canseco started the fight by throwing two jabs that missed. Sikahema responded with a hard left that connected with Canseco's jaw. "His pupils dilated," said Sikahema in an interview. (I'm sorry, but that quote is funny as hell.)

Canseco dropped to the mat after only thirty seconds. After struggling to recover, Canseco got up, and Sikahema pounded away. Canseco had no clue how to defend himself. It was like stealing steroids from a baby. "Whatever size advantage he had, it was negated by his stupidity," said Sikahema. (I'm sorry, but that quote is funny as hell, too.)

The fight was over in 97 seconds. Ninety-seven freaking seconds. "I read him right from jump-street," said Sikahema. "He's soft inside. I think he was probably physically imposing his entire life and he intimidated people. So he didn't have to fight. I bet you he's never fought in his life. I had that sense he's never been in a scrap, so I was going to hit him in the mouth and see what happened."

This fight utterly obliterated what was left of Canseco's already frail image. At one point, he was the spark that ignited the search for steroid truths in baseball. There was something admirable about that. He has quickly lost that luster and is now more pathetic. Following that ass-beating, he's just laughable. Afterward, Canseco made a bevy of excuses for losing to Sikahema, including a claim he had food poisoning. What he had was Sikahema poisoning.

Most of these types of celebrity boxing matches are silly and buffoonish. Send in the clowns. This one was different. How can you not love to see the little guy who works in Philly win over the big-mouth rat? It's a real-life Rocky story. More importantly, Sikahema proved something I've been saying for some time. Most people have no idea how much skill it takes to box competently. Many professional athletes, ego oozing from their pores, think they can step into a ring and take on a skilled fighter with the same kind of ease as pulling a popsicle out of the freezer. Canseco has claimed black belts in Taekwondo, Kung Fu, and Muay Thai, along with some twenty years of martial arts experience. He'd planned on beginning a mixed martial arts career after the Sikahema fight. He failed to understand just how tough Sikahema was.

If you have been around Philadelphia for any amount of time in the past few decades, you know the name Sikahema. Before he became a television journalist, he was a Pro Bowl special-teams player in the NFL for eight seasons—including a stint with the Eagles—who would punch the goalposts in a fury after a score. Sikahema has been boxing since he was a kid and had more than 80 amateur bouts. He once fought in a Golden Gloves title match, losing to Sugar Ray Leonard (no shame in that since many people did). Sikahema trained for six rounds, and Canseco trained with

Anti-Jerks

The top 10 good guys (and gals) in sports history, otherwise known as the anti-jerks:

10. **Mary Carillo** – Was a friendly person as a professional tennis player and hasn't changed as a television analyst.

9. **David Robinson** – Once told me, "I feel terrible when I blow off an autograph seeker. I even feel bad when I blow off the media." Always has a smile on his face.

8. **Lisa Leslie** – Maybe the best basketball player in Olympic history, she has won four gold medals and will also go down as one of the top three players in WNBA history. Yet Leslie has never gotten full of herself.

7. **Mario Lemieux** – Beat Hodgkin's, corresponded with others who suffered from that disease, then contributed $5 million to the Pittsburgh Medical Center Health System. He's also raised millions for Hodgkin's disease research.

6. **A.C. Green** – Played in the NBA and never succumbed to the temptation of having dozens of girlfriends. In fact, spent much of his young life as a virgin. Very un-jerk like.

5. **Bobby Bowden** – There has never been a more gentle and accessible coach.

4. **Jackie Robinson** – Never became bitter or angry over how he was treated while breaking baseball's color line.

3 **Dikembe Mutombo** – Has spent and generated millions of dollars to improve conditions in his native Republic of Congo. Was invited to speak at President George W. Bush's State of the Union address in 2007.

2. **Julie Foudy** – Has long been an advocate for women and children. She launched the Julie Foudy Sports Leadership Academy for young girls.

1. **Warrick Dunn** – Has helped dozens of single mothers purchase homes by providing them with the down payment.

six beers. It was a mismatch, indeed. The big guy was destined to get knocked out.

Here's another nice part of this story. Sikahema took some of his winnings and donated them to the widow of a slain Philadelphia police officer. "I was fighting for a cause," Sikahema said. "I'm not sure what he was fighting for." I'm not sure, either. I'm not sure Canseco knew. He's a lost soul and a beaten man in more ways than one.

Unlike Sikahema, the anti-jerk.

In a fitting end for Canseco, Joe Martinez, the county commissioner in Canseco's hometown of Miami, offered a resolution in September 2008 to have Canseco's named removed from the street it's been on for two decades.

Chicago Black Sox

It's possible the Chicago Black Sox deserve to be much higher on the jerk scale. After all, they intentionally lost the 1919 World Series, one of the great despicable acts in sports history. Yet the Black Sox scandal occurred almost a century ago, and not even one of the more notorious groups of jerks can stop the withering effects of time. Okay, so that's bull malarkey, but it sounded all smart and stuff, right?

While time has indeed taken some of the edge off what was once considered perhaps the greatest sports scandal ever, what the Black Sox did still resonates today. The Black Sox are the biggest reason why gambler Pete Rose, all-time great and jerk immortal, isn't in the Hall of Fame. Rose is one of the most

Outfielder Joseph "Shoeless Joe" Jackson ended his 14 seasons in the majors with a lifetime batting average of .356. He played in the majors from 1908 to 1920. He was one of the key figures in the infamous "Black Sox" scandal, which rocked baseball and caused the introduction of a baseball commissioner. (AP photo)

prolific players baseball has ever seen, but his gambling on the Cincinnati Reds tarnished every hit and hustle. The banishment of Rose traces directly back to the Black Sox.

Many sports fans have forgotten just how diabolically clever the Black Sox players were and how easily the scandal could've been prevented. The player who served as the centrifuge of the scandal, first baseman Arnold Gandil, had years-long relationships with various gangsters and petty criminals. Players on the team weren't shy in discussing their desires to fix the series. The talk of a rigged World Series became so boisterous that serious gamblers flooded Cincinnati, the opponent of the White Sox, with cash, and that in turn caused the odds against Cincinnati to dramatically fall. Certain members of the Chicago press had their suspicions, as well. Baseball seemed mostly unaware, but the clues were indeed there.

Eight White Sox players were banned. Claude Williams lost three games in that World Series, an incredible feat as only one other player in World Series history has ever lost that many contests, further suggesting the fix was in. While there has since been some doubt about his role in the scandal, Joe Jackson was also banned. Gandil, Oscar Felsch, Eddie Cicotte, Charles Risberg, Fred McMullin, and George Weaver were the others.

While the scandal is distant history, it still remains extremely jerk-worthy as a cautionary note. It's startling how, despite books being written about the scandal (as well as a movie made about it) and its anchor-deep setting in popular culture, athletes still secretly bet on games. Rose and others never learned from the Black Sox scandal. What's even more frightening is that there's probably a player who has still failed to heed the warning. Some athlete is betting on a game as you read this and making him or herself future jerk material in the process.

Tatum Bell

Y ou may notice when we're discussing Tatum Bell, lots of fancy lawyer words like "alleged" and "allegedly" and "allegedly alleged." That cautious language allows a discussion for the stunning case of NFL player Tatum Bell.

In professional sports, the locker room and clubhouse are viewed as pseudo-sanctuaries. It's an asinine and narcissistic

Detroit Lions running back Tatum Bell picks up three yards on a run against the Cleveland Browns in the first quarter of an NFL preseason football game on Saturday, August 18, 2007, in Cleveland. (AP Photo/ Mark Duncan)

belief, but it's a fact. There is one thing seen by athletes as more treasonous than putting itching powder in a jockstrap: stealing from a teammate. That's allegedly—there's that word again— what Bell did.

The entire insane story starts with the Detroit Lions signing running back Rudi Johnson and releasing Bell. Johnson claimed that while on his way out of the locker room, Bell stole two of his bags. When the bags were returned, Johnson said they were missing his identification, $200 in cash, credit cards, and underwear. Not certain what's worse, stealing another man's cash or pilfering his underwear, especially if it was just freshly washed (the underwear, not the cash). "All this happened once he got released," Johnson told the media. "He came here to get some stuff out of his locker. That's when he scooped the bags up. Some real shyster, conniving stuff, man."

Damn straight it is. Allegedly. Bell claimed the entire episode was a simple mistake. "I ain't no thief," Bell told the *Detroit Free Press.* "I ain't never been one, and I ain't never going to be one. It was all a misunderstanding. You can ask anybody I played with for all my years or anybody that know me, man. They know I ain't never stolen nothing from nobody or had those kind of intentions." Somewhere Bell's grammar school teacher is composing her own jerk list, and Bell is near the top.

There were two versions of what occurred. Johnson claims he left the bags in the locker room then proceeded to leave temporarily and speak to then team president Matt Millen (speaking of stealing money—Millen did that as Lions team president for years). The bags were Gucci. Well, of course they were. When Johnson returned, the Gucci beauties were gone. A member of the team security staff showed Johnson a tape and allegedly on it, according to Johnson, was Bell making off with the bags. This story is either perfect jerk material or the next Jason Bourne sequel.

Missing were Perry Ellis boxers. Well, of course they were. Bell claimed it was all just one, big, videotaped misunderstanding. He doesn't wear Perry Ellis. He's a Fruit of the Loom guy. "If you look on film, I wasn't in no hurry or nothing," Bell said. "I was just going about my day. I tried to talk to Rudi...but he was pretty upset, so I let it go. So now it's that I'm being a thief. I come to found out that the bags weren't whose I thought they was. It was just an honest mistake, man." (Grammar teacher slaps herself upside the head again. One thing is perfectly clear: Bell certainly didn't pilfer Johnson's grammar book.)

We all make mistakes. We are all at times Jerky McJerks. Stealing from someone? Just after you were cut from the team? Taking their underwear? Perry Ellis underwear for God's sake? Terrorism, global warming, and now skivvy thievery. Is there no decency left in the world?

Allegedly.

96   Drew Rosenhaus

The slicked-back hair, the loud mouth, the grandstanding, the petulance, the rabid obnoxiousness, and the self-importance. All of those things are the embodiment of agent Drew Rosenhaus.

"A first class jackass," said an NFL general manager who asked not to be identified. Well, mom always said to be the best at everything.

"One of the worst people in our business," said an NFL coach. One? One?

"He's Drew Rosenjerk," said another general manager.

Swear on the Jerk Bible that's a true quote. Unbelievably perfect.

Rosenhaus represents one of the significant things dramatically wrong with professional sports (and to some degree college sports, as well): agents.

Agents are a necessary part of the process. They prevent teams from abusing their power, and agents were also a pivotal part of increasing salaries and the rights of players in the NFL, the most physically brutal of the professional sports. Most agents are good men and women who have only the best interests of their clients at heart. Rosenhaus may as well, but he's reached hall of fame jerk levels because it seems he's increasingly put his own interests and überdesire to sign (some rival agents say steal) every NFL client who has two functioning legs and working arms to his company. More than anything, it seems that self-promotion is now Rosenhaus' main job description. He's not alone in the agent universe at doing this, but he's probably at the top of the list.

Rosenhaus and one of his clients, Terrell Owens (Jerk No. 29), caused a near implosion of the entire Philadelphia team when Owens was an Eagle. The fight between Rosenhaus and the Eagles got so ugly that it ruined the team's post–Super Bowl appearance in 2005. Rosenhaus and Owens basically decided to do the following: Owens was going to act like such a jerk it would leave the Eagles no choice but to get rid of him, and that's exactly what occurred. Owens acted like a petulant chump doing sit-ups in his driveway with cameras rolling, getting into altercations with teammates, and showing public disrespect to the coaching staff and front office. All of his behavior was facilitated by Rosenhaus if not encouraged.

Rosenhaus wasn't done with the Eagles. In 2008, years after his first dance with the team, Rosenhaus surfaced in a video in which he blasted the Eagles for treating his client, Lito Sheppard, poorly. The Eagles were paying Sheppard $2 million a year. If that's malicious treatment, then we here at the Jerk Council wouldn't mind being mistreated that way seven days a week.

Rosenhaus also mocked the player who was starting over Sheppard—a defensive back named Sheldon Brown. When Brown heard about Rosenhaus' backhand slap, he responded accordingly. "I don't know [Rosenhaus] personally," Brown said. "I just take care of my business. I don't want [anyone] in my business, and I don't want to be in anybody else's business. That's how me and my agent handle things. [Rosenhaus] doesn't scout for the Eagles. Does he know how many passes I defend or intercept in practice? That's part of the game. So nothing he says has worth."

This is part of the Rosenhaus personality that seems to constantly rear its jerk head and why he's so jerk-worthy. It just seems like Rosenhaus is more concerned about feeding his ego than anything else.

95 Mike Gundy

To fully understand the jerk nature of Oklahoma State football coach Mike Gundy, it's imperative to first digest what might be the greatest coaching rant we've ever seen. Here's the rant transcribed in its entirety. Please make sure the kids have left the room before reading.

Gundy was irritated over a newspaper article that featured claims about one of the Oklahoma State players. He held the story in his hand as he started to scream and belittle the female journalist who wrote it.

"Three-fourths of this is inaccurate," Gundy began. "It's fiction. And this article embarrasses me to be involved with athletics. Tremendously. And that article had to have been written by a person who didn't have a child. And has never had a child that had their *heart broken* and come home upset. And had to deal with that child when he is upset. And kick a person when he's down! Here's all that kid did. He goes to class. He's respectful to the media. He's respectful to the *public*. And he's a good kid, and he's not a professional athlete, and he doesn't deserve to be kicked when he's down.

"If you have a child someday, you'll understand how it feels. But you obviously don't have a child. I do. If your child goes down the street, and someone makes fun of him because he dropped a pass in a pickup game, or *says he's fat*, and he comes home crying to his mom, you'd understand. But you haven't had that. But someday you will. And when your child comes home, you'll understand. If you want to go at an athlete, *one of my athletes*, you go after one that doesn't do the right things. You don't downgrade him because he does everything right and may not play as well on Saturday. And you let us make that decision. That's why I don't read the newspaper. *Because it's garbage.* And the editor that let it come out is *garbage*. Attacking an amateur athlete for doing everything right. And then you want to write articles about guys that don't do things right, and downgrade those who do make plays. Are you kidding me? Where are we at in society?"

This is where Gundy gives the money quote that will be played again and again for years to come: *"COME AFTER ME! I'M A MAN! I'M FORTY!"*

He continued, "I'm not a kid. Write something about me or our coaches. Don't write it about a kid that does everything right. That's [how a] heart is broken. And then say that the coaches said he was scared. *That ain't true.* And then to say that we made that decision because Donovan was…because he threatened to transfer. *That's not true.* So get your facts straight. And I hope someday you have a child and someone downgrades him or belittles him, and you have to look him in the eye and say you know what? It's okay. They're supposed to be mature adults but they really aren't. Who's the kid? Who's the kid here? Are you kidding me? That's all I got to say. Makes me wanna puke!"

Well, okay then. Where do we begin? With the inappropriateness of lecturing a career-oriented woman journalist about not having children? The bullying misogyny of a man screaming at a woman? The fact that much of the story was indeed quite accurate? Gundy receives multiple jerk bonuses. The rant by Gundy demonstrates the increasing thin-skinned nature of coaches. Many coaches, particularly in college and professional football, have long been psycho control freaks, and they've justified their occasionally obnoxious behavior by blaming the intense desire (but often unwarranted desire) for secrecy in the sport. Some of the irritability with the coaches and the public is understandable. The Internet and access to massive amounts of information gives an ordinary person the belief that they know as much as the coaches, and this frustrates them as fans post harsh opinions on message boards and media members take their criticisms and rips to blogs.

Gundy, however, crossed the line. Not only did he prey on the complicated feelings and guilt of working women who don't have children, Gundy had little factual basis for his Nikita Khrushchev–like rant.

Perhaps most relevant of all—is *that* the type of example you want to set for young athletes? That you respond to disagreements with hysterical rants?

At the Jerk Council, we have a dream. One day that reporter will get to say to Gundy, "I have a child now, and he's going to Oklahoma."

Top 10 Best Rants Ever

10. Kellen Winslow, Jr., tight end for the Cleveland Browns – Proclaimed he was a soldier.

9. Herm Edwards, coach of the Kansas City Chiefs – "Hello! You play...to win...the game."

8. John Chaney, Temple coach – Threatened to beat the hell out of coach John Calipari.

7. Hal McRae, former Kansas City Royals manager – Breaks new tirade ground by having a breakdown in his underwear.

6. Lee Elia, former Chicago Cubs manager – Became extremely angered by fans booing the club. Probably the most foul-mouthed rant ever. And we mean...ever. Set a new record for the use of the word f---, motherf-----, and coc-------. Also ripped fans by saying, "85 percent of the world is working. The other 15 come out here."

5. Dan Hawkins, Colorado Buffaloes coach – Go play intramurals, brother.

4. Gundy – No tirade before his ever featured someone declaring their age and gender.

3. Allen Iverson, Denver Nuggets player – Talking 'bout practice!

2. Jim Mora, former Indianapolis head coach – His playoffs rant has become the stuff of legend.

1. Dennis Green, former Arizona head coach – Easily, without question, the funniest rant ever thanks to the phrase, "They are who we thought they were."

Phil Jackson

Phil Jackson isn't your typical jerk. There are many excellent and redeeming qualities about the Los Angeles Lakers coach. He's remarkably intelligent and thoughtful. We ask our athletes and coaches to consider aspects of life other than ta-tas, signing bonuses, and more ta-tas. Jackson does that. There is an introspective part to his personality. Plus, he's dated the owner's daughter. There's something both jerky and boldly delicious about him getting away with that.

The problem is the smug factor. It's remarkably high. Phil Jackson makes Tiki Barber look like Mahatma Gandhi. The line between smugness and confidence is thin, but Jackson crosses it with stunts designed to make himself look like the smartest person in the gym. He uses words like *haberdashery* and *antanaclasis* just because he can. Anyone who relishes in the artificial moniker "the Zen Master" takes smugness to new oxygen-challenged heights.

What he did in 2000 is an example. Prior to playing the Sacramento Kings in the opening round of the postseason, Jackson attempted to motivate his players with a little film splicing. It wasn't the first time Jackson had used the popular media to motivate his teams, but this time he used the movie *American History X*. The film stars Edward Norton as a former neo-Nazi thug. What does that have to do with basketball? Well…ah…well…thinking— absolutely nothing. This didn't stop Jackson from making what was a completely inappropriate comparison utilizing *American History X*. Jackson took players from the opposing Kings team and

Los Angeles Lakers coach Phil Jackson complains about a call during the second quarter of Game 2 of the NBA basketball finals against the Boston Celtics on Sunday, June 8, 2008, in Boston. (AP Photo/Winslow Townson)

juxtaposed their images with Nazi characters from the film. Jackson had to know what he was doing. He was showing a mostly African American locker room images of Nazis. Then, to make things worse, Jackson compared the Sacramento coach to Adolf Hitler. It was a disgraceful act, and Jackson never truly publicly apologized for it.

He did apologize in November 2007 when he stated after a Lakers loss to San Antonio that the game was a *"Brokeback Mountain* game because there's so much penetration and kickouts."* It was a reference to the 2005 movie about two male cowboys and their affair. Yet even in his apology, Jackson couldn't resist the urge to show his inner jerk. "If I've offended any horses, Texans, cowboys, or gays, I apologize," Jackson said.

Okay, that was funny. Jerky, but funny.

Here's what's also funny. Jackson has coached Michael Jordan, Shaquille O'Neal, Kobe Bryant, and Scottie Pippen. Jackson has won numerous titles, but your niece could coach that group and she wouldn't use skinhead movies to motivate them, either.

 # Steve Smith

If you are a teammate of Carolina Panthers wide receiver Steve Smith, watch your back. Watch your face. Watch your jaw, specifically. Watch everything, because Smith has the same control of his temper as Robert De Niro's Al Capone character in *The Untouchables.*

It seems Smith has teeny-tiny little issues with some teammates. You see, he's beat the crap out of two of them. Stone-cold whipped their asses. For what? We're not exactly certain and it's not clear even if Smith knows why the hell he pounded their faces in. He just did it because he could. (Please don't hit anyone on the Jerk Council if you see this, Steve. We bruise easily.)

Fights between teammates have occurred in football since the beginning of the sport. In the early 1900s, there were more

brawls than passes. In more civilized times, we tend to frown
on such things. Admittedly, it's somewhat hypocritical for fans
and the media to cheer the violence of professional football—in
which players are regularly concussed and possibly have their
lives dramatically shortened by unbelievable physical trauma—
while looking down their noses at fights in practice. Yet Smith has
twice crossed a line. The line is thin, but it's there.

The most recent Smith brawl happened in the summer of 2008
during Carolina's training camp. Smith and Carolina teammate Ken
Lucas were mouthing off to one another in practice, then suddenly
there was a scrum. Or so it seemed. The problem is it's unclear if
Lucas was prepared for a brawl or even facing Smith when Smith
punched him. What is clear is that Lucas suffered a broken nose,
and the Panthers suspended Smith for two games.

The first time Smith lost his temper happened six years earlier.
He punched teammate Anthony Bright in the face during a film
session. How angry a person do you have to be to punch someone
out during a film session? Imagine how that session must have gone.

Bright: "Steve, I think that defense is going to play a lot of
cover-two against you."

Smith: *"What the hell did you say?"*

Bright: "I just said the defense is going to play cover-two."

Smith: *"Cover-two? You're talking about my momma, aren't
you?"*

Bright: "No, no. I was talking about cover-two. What does that
have to do with your momma?"

Smith: *"Oh, I see, so now you're saying my momma can't play
cover-two? Get ready for a beat-down, Mr. Bright."*

Bright got the last laugh. He sued Smith, and the lawsuit
was settled out of court. There's no truth to the talk that Smith
punched the judge presiding over the case.

Hot Tempers

*Five Sports Figures You Don't Want to Get Angry…
You Wouldn't Like Them When They're Angry.*

5. **Jeremy Foley** – The athletic director at Florida known to verbally abuse media members who write anything remotely critical of the Gator program.

4. **Tony Stewart** – Hair-trigger temper on the track.

3. **Bill Romanowski** – Spit at a player, punched a teammate in the eye and crushed his eye socket, among many other incidents.

2. **John Daly** – Twice accused of physically attacking women. Not the charmer some suckers think he is.

1. **Bob Knight** – Might be the most mal-tempered sports personality we've ever seen. Not sure who we'd take in a Steve Smith–Knight boxing match.

92 Arlen Specter

It is difficult to call a highly intelligent United States Senator who has done so much for his country—and he's a cancer survivor, to boot—a jerk. Yet this is why we on the Jerk Council get the big bucks and make the tough decisions. Specter's career is remarkable, but he's done one thing that's landed him on this highly prestigious list. He played politics with professional football.

Sure, being political and manipulative is like foreplay in Washington, and the mix of politics and sports practically goes back to medieval times. Specter's conduct will go down as one of the worst examples of this, and it's all related to Spygate.

New England coach Bill Belichick's well-documented flirtation with video cameras led to one of the more fascinating sports moments of the 2007–08 season. Specter raised a public stink when the NFL destroyed the photographic evidence of the Patriots taping the signals of opposing teams. Specter's concern on the surface seems legitimate. While the NFL maintained there was little on the tapes already not generally known, Specter smelled a rat (no, not Eric Mangini). He publicly questioned both the NFL's motive and integrity. It was extremely passionate and interesting stuff.

The problem was that Specter had what many believed—including the Jerk Council—was a conflict of interest. Specter's noble battle with football wasn't exactly so noble. Specter is first a huge Philadelphia Eagles fan, and the Patriots defeated the Eagles in Super Bowl XXXIX. So Specter likely had a built-in dislike of the Patriots to start. It doesn't cease there. What Specter initially never discussed was that his beef with the NFL might have deeper roots. The NFL and the cable television behemoth Comcast were in a heated dispute over the distribution of the NFL Network. According to various published reports, Comcast has been a major contributor to Specter's campaign to the tune of hundreds of thousands of dollars. Ohhhhh, now it all makes sense.

Of course Specter was going to annoy the NFL because the NFL was annoying Specter by fighting with one of Specter's largest contributors.

Patriots fans became enraged, besieging Specter's office with numerous complaints. There were newspaper and website editorials criticizing Specter. Some within the Patriots organization remain infuriated to this day by Specter's actions, and while Specter is a heroic figure overall, what he did in this case was nothing short of an abuse of power.

College Football Fans

This selection is the first group pick because that's how we roll here at the Jerk Council. Sometimes, people behave so jerkified they deserve to be corralled into one large group of...jerks. They're special, like a rare disease. That's what you have with some college football fans (emphasis on some—Ivy League fans are well behaved). As Foxsports.com wrote when it ranked the most obnoxious fan bases: "[These fans] live in the past and never shut up. They're sore losers and worse winners. Blackboard, meet fingernails." This is the first jerks-within-the-jerks presentation, so without further delay, here are the top ten worst college football fan bases. Hurry and read it before a West Virginia fan throws a beer bottle at your head.

10. Ohio State

Once made death threats to a teaching assistant who rightly ratted on then-beloved running back Maurice Clarett for receiving special treatment from at least one professor. Death threats to a teaching assistant? That might be worse than when Philly fans booed Santa Claus.

9. University of Florida

There was a joke about former Gator coach Steve Spurrier that went like this.

Question: What's the difference between God and Steve Spurrier?

Answer: God doesn't think he's Steve Spurrier.

The arrogance of Spurrier carried downward to the Gator fan base. Now, not only are Gator fans arrogant, they're belligerent. Started Fireronzook.com, take pride in intimidating media members and curtailing free speech, and made more than 200 threatening phone calls (some several dozen of them death threats) to a tow-truck operator who notified police when a Gator player attempted to forcibly remove a vehicle that belonged to the player's girlfriend from the tow lot. No one puts the "M" in mob like the Gators.

8. Clemson

At least Ohio State and Florida have won multiple championships in football. In the past decade, Clemson has as many Division I national titles as Dartmouth, yet the Tigers act like they've won like John Wooden's UCLA Bruins. Calm down, Tigers.

7. West Virginia

When Bobby Bowden, the classy and genteel former West Virginia coach, had several seasons where the team struggled, he saw his likeness hung in effigy one day. Fast-forward to the messy departure of former Mountaineer coach Rich Rodriguez to Michigan. Some West Virginia fans behaved almost inhumanely, threatening physical harm to members of the Rodriguez family. It got so bad that Rodriguez's mother, Arleen, wrote an op-ed piece for the Fairmont Times–West Virginian newspaper. It read in part, "It was deplorable that our family, especially the children, have been threatened and property damaged..."

6. Oklahoma

Constantly overestimate the greatness of their teams. Year after year after year.

5. Michigan

Perhaps whine more than any fans in college football and are still complaining about their team's drop in the rankings after a 2006 loss to top-ranked Ohio State.

4. Tennessee

The Jerk Council truly believes that if former coach Phil Fulmer was caught in bed with a barnyard animal, fans would still support him. Not all fans, but many.

3. Notre Dame

Not even the fact that their program has absolutely stunk under Charlie Weiss has quelled the arrogance of the Irish fan.

2. University of Alabama

Absolute, definitive nut jobs.

1. Auburn University

In general, football fans living in the South totally lose perspective. Auburn fans exemplify this.

You'll have to excuse the Jerk Council while we run out to the street and make sure no football fan is burning a couch.

James L. Dolan

This about Jim Dolan from *Sports Illustrated*'s S.L. Price, "The tales of Jim's drug-and-drink-addled past, his volcanic temper, his shifting moods, were already legendary, fueling the image of a spoiled boy who had been handed the keys to perhaps the most prized property in all of U.S. sports..." That property would be the New York Knicks, and there are few examples in the history of professional sports where the ruination of a franchise can be traced back to practically one person. In this case, that person is Dolan.

When the Knicks were slammed with a sexual harassment lawsuit and subsequently ordered to pay $11.6 million in damages to plaintiff Anucha Browne Sanders, the league's commissioner, David Stern, had seen enough. He was so disappointed at the state of the Knicks that he issued a damning statement to ESPN. Asked what the harassment case indicated about the state of the franchise, Stern told ESPN, "It demonstrates that they're not a model of intelligent management. There were many checkpoints along the way where more decisive action would have eliminated this issue."

The Knicks? Not a model of intelligent management? That would be the understatement of the twenty-first century. That's like saying Enron wasn't a model of intelligent management. Though Dolan heads other sports properties (most notably the New York Rangers), it's what he's done to the Knicks that's the most devastating, and in many ways, it's sad to watch as one of the proudest franchises in the history of sports is ground to dust under Dolan's loafers.

It's difficult to state what's been Dolan's biggest mistake because he's made a number of them. His strained relationship with Dave Checketts led to Checketts departing. While Checketts wasn't perfect, he was the captain of Madison Square Garden during its most successful period ever, an era that saw the Rangers win a championship and the Knicks make annual and deep postseason runs. The Knicks went from that to Isiah Thomas, who built a payroll that climbed to more than $100 million and got nothing for it except what Price called, "perhaps the most spectacularly awful year in NBA history." That was 2006. That was after the Larry Brown disaster. That was after the Knicks and Denver Nuggets engaged in an ugly brawl. That was after Stephon Marbury first feuded with Brown and then Thomas.

To say the Knicks have been a soap opera under Dolan would be an insult to soap operas. The Knicks are all opera and no soap. Not exactly sure what that means, but somehow it makes sense.

The NBA would love for Dolan to either wise up or go away, likely more the latter than the former. Unfortunately, it seems Dolan is here to stay for some time as the Knicks sink further into the abyss.

 # Jerramy Stevens

This is terribly exciting because we get to introduce our first true Jerk Thug in the rankings. Jerk Thugs (copyright 2009) are different from your pedestrian jerks. Regular jerks date eight

---

Best Sports Owners

The Five Best Owners in Sports History (The Anti-Dolans)

5. Wellington Mara, late owner of the New York Giants – One of the great leaders in football history and a key figure in taking the NFL from its prehistoric beginnings to its billion-dollar glossiness.

4. Dan Rooney, Pittsburgh Steelers – One of the few people in professional sports who is always honest.

3. Robert Kraft, New England Patriots – Could easily be the top dog.

2. Jerry Buss, Los Angeles Lakers – While he mishandled the Shaquille O'Neal v. Kobe Bryant feud, Buss is one of the greatest winners in sports history.

1. George Steinbrenner, Yankees – Might simultaneously be the most hated and the best. To some, he represents the worst in sports—to others, like us here at the Jerk Council, he doesn't hoard his lucrative television revenues. He spends almost every dollar he can on teams.

One last thing on top owners—no list would be complete without Mark Cuban, owner of the Dallas Mavericks. But this is only a top five list. If it was a top ten list, Cuban would be on it.

---

women at once. Jerk Thugs date eight women and beat up four others. Regular jerks pray for a misdemeanor. Jerk Thugs think a felony will increase their credit score. Regular jerks bring a knife to a gunfight. Jerk Thugs bring a gun, some cocaine, two ex-strippers, and their defense attorney to a gunfight.

There are only a few athletes who personify the Jerk Thug better than Jerramy Stevens. Based on newspaper and Internet reports as well as court documents read by the author, a disturbing portrait of Stevens emerges. It's a story of a player

Seattle Seahawks tight end Jerramy Stevens addressed a news conference on Thursday, February 2, 2006, in Dearborn, Michigan. Stevens incensed Steelers linebacker Jerry Porter earlier that week, saying Jerome Bettis' return to his hometown (Detroit) wouldn't have a happy ending. The Seahawks lost Super Bowl XL to the Pittsburgh Steelers. (AP Photo/Elaine Thompson)

who received numerous chances because of his talent. This is not a new phenomenon, but in Stevens' case, the creative excuse-making by college and professional teams on his behalf seemed to have reached new heights.

Stevens' arrest record is impressive. It's so impressive that it makes O.J. Simpson jealous. It begins in June 1998 when he was arrested for second- and fourth-degree assault. Stevens was accused of beating up a 17-year-old victim and ending the fight by kicking the alleged victim in the face. He pled guilty to misdemeanor assault. One month after that, he was drug tested and failed for marijuana. Two years after that, he was arrested for sexually assaulting a college student. No charges were filed, but the woman did sue Stevens and received a financial settlement.

At this point, there was more than enough evidence to demonstrate that Stevens was a hazard and teams should have stayed as far away as possible from him. That didn't happen. The University of Washington stuck by Stevens, as did the Seattle Seahawks—and Stevens wasn't done enhancing his criminal resume just yet. In 2001, Stevens pled guilty to a hit-and-run and was sentenced to 240 hours of community service. Stevens crashed his car into a nursing home building. Just 23 months later, Stevens was again accused of driving while drunk and reckless driving. He spent two days in jail and paid a fine. In March 2007, after his third drunk-driving charge in less than six years, a jury found him guilty of the accusation and he spent 12 days in jail.

It took a long, long while, but even the highly tolerant Seahawks had seen enough of their precious Jerk Thug. They released him. You know where this is headed, right? One man's jerk is another man's Jerk Thug. The Tampa Bay Buccaneers signed Stevens after the Seahawks dropped him. That's correct. After all those arrests, he got another chance, and as a Buccaneer he didn't disappoint. Stevens was suspended for two games for violating the league's substance abuse policy as a result of his 2007 arrest.

Considering the massive number of chances Stevens received from teams, it's fair to wonder who is the true Jerk Thug in this case? Is it Stevens or the teams that continue to employ him?

Marty McSorley

"You can't make a guy a tough guy."
—MARTY MCSORLEY

There are various highlight reels of Marty McSorley fighting. Marty McSorley fighting is as normal as teenage rebellion. McSorley vs. Bob Probert. McSorley vs. Tim Hunter. McSorley vs. Eric Lindros. On and on it goes. If it were possible when McSorley was still playing, he would've fought Mike Tyson.

"What a battle between two heavyweights," the game announcer says in one particular fight.

The hockey community celebrated McSorley for his fight skills until a disastrous day on February 21, 2000. McSorley was playing for the Boston Bruins when everything changed for him and, in some ways, the entire sport. McSorley smashed his stick into the helmeted head of Donald Brashear, and Brashear fell backward. His head landed hard on the ice, and Brashear was knocked unconscious almost instantly.

The hit became news around the entire world, especially after McSorley was charged with assault. The National Hockey League suspended McSorley for the entire season; and later, the suspension was amended to an entire year. He was later found guilty of assault with a weapon and never played in the NHL again.

McSorley's place in jerk history is assured. Beat a guy with a stick, knock him unconscious with a Grade 3 concussion, and jerkdom status is a certainty. Yet there's an interesting dichotomy

Top Five Goons of All Time

5. Gordie Howe – There's actually a phrase called the "Gordie Howe hat-trick." It involves a goal, an assist, and a brawl all in one game. Very nice.

4. Dave Schultz – When you are part of a team called the "Broad Street Bullies," then you fit right in as a goon. It also doesn't hurt when your nickname is "The Hammer."

3. Dave Semenko – Had as good a jab as George Foreman and basically played the role of protector for Wayne Gretzky.

2. Shane Churla – Took pride in how battered his face would occasionally get.

1. Tiger Williams – A very arguable choice here as there are other solid candidates for the top spot, but Williams shattered many NHL records for penalty minutes.

at work when it comes to McSorley and other hockey goons. Indeed, hockey fans and the sport in general almost deserve co-jerk status. The at-times ugly and over-the-top violence on the ice is accepted by fans and declared part of the sport. There's almost a sense of romanticism with goons who are seen as protectors. It's a twisted logic, particularly considering some of those same fans will blast NBA players as thugs and punks when they get into brawls.

This isn't to defend fighting in basketball or any other sport. There's simply a great deal of hypocrisy—and racial undertones—when the McSorleys are defended as warriors when they brawl and NBA players are blasted as criminals when they do. Shouldn't society disown all fighting in team sports? Is that so crazy?

Minnesota Vikings Sex Boaters

Sex in public. With hookers flown in from Atlanta and Florida. Sex in public on a boat, no less (actually is there any other kind of sex?). Then, as an attorney for the cruise ship where these alleged acts took place noted, some of the various sexy-McSexyness included "masturbation, oral sex, anal sex, woman on man, woman on woman, man on man, toys, double penetration, middle of the floor, middle of the couches, middle of the room." Sounds exactly like my honeymoon.

Seriously, the only thing missing from the Minnesota Vikings Sex Boat Scandal were barnyard animals and Leprechauns.

Sometimes, the jerks make it far too easy.

What kind of hubris does it take for a large group of athletes to rent several cruise ship–type boats, fill them with almost 100 people, and then some of the players proceed to perform sex acts in front of the crew members? Did some of the Minnesota Vikings players actually believe crew members wanted to see their nastiness? Watching players with prostitutes…ewwwww.

This is not to say that group sex has never happened before. Sex parties have likely occurred in every frat house in the country, so there shouldn't be, in some ways, a double standard. It's also likely the Vikings were being made an example. The Sex Boaters, however, went a step too far. They were having sex in front of people who wanted no part of the action. It was boorish and arrogant. The partiers also left behind their—ahem—tools of the trade. Published reports at the time of the incident in October 2005 stated that the cleaning crew found used

Celebrity Sex Scandals

Five Famous Cases Involving Celebrities and Sex Scandals

5. George Michael – Arrested in 1998 for engaging in a lewd act in a public bathroom in Beverly Hills, California. Didn't even know Beverly Hills had public bathrooms, but they're probably the cleanest in the nation.

4. Hugh Grant – Arrested for lewd conduct in a public place after being caught with a prostitute named Divine Brown. Hugh and Divine…sounds like a Hollywood street intersection.

3. Marv Albert – In 1997 was accused of biting a woman and wearing women's underwear. Let's be honest, fellas. Raise your hand if you've ever tried on a woman's bra. No hands raised? Liars!

2. Paul Reubens – Caught publicly masturbating in an adult theatre in 1991. The movie Reubens was watching was *Nurse Nancy*. Would've made a better story if he were watching the NFL Network.

1. R. Kelly – Found not guilty in 2008 of videotaping himself having sex with an underage girl. Video cameras should only be utilized to film the signals of opposing coaches.

condoms, K-Y Jelly, Handi Wipes, and wrappers for sex toys. Wait. Sex toys have wrappers? Or maybe they meant rappers with sex toys.

The scandal happened years ago, and to this day it's difficult to tell exactly which Vikings players were involved, but initially four were charged with indecent conduct, lewd or lascivious conduct, and disorderly conduct—in others words, the perfect jerk trifurcate. Moe Williams was found guilty on a single count of disorderly conduct. Fred Smoot and Bryant McKinnie pled guilty to misdemeanor disorderly conduct. They were also fined by the NFL, which apparently stands for the No Flotation League.

There hasn't been a sex boat case since then and it's unlikely there ever will be again. Players probably learned a valuable lesson. There's nothing like a good hotel room.

86 DeSean Jackson

R arely are people given the privilege of making this prestigious list at a young age, but one man has done exactly that. Philadelphia Eagles wide receiver DeSean Jackson is going to end up as a cautionary tale. He absolutely will. Twenty years from now, some coach will say to some hot-dogging fool, "If you keep this up, you're going to end up like DeSean Jackson." And that won't be viewed as a good thing.

Sadly, Jackson is likely a lost cause. He clearly doesn't listen to anyone and could give a damn about how he's viewed, which are two dangerous aspects of his personality. He's practically destined to jackass himself out of football (yeah, the Jerk Council used jackass that way). Then he'll look back and wonder what the hell happened.

There have been people in Jackson's ear for some time now. "DeSean, calm down," they've told him. "DeSean, you're a great talent, let your ability speak for itself." Unfortunately, Jackson might never get it, and he's part of a larger issue, one in which too many African American players seem to have no problem Steppin' and Fetchin' before America without guilt or shame. The Jerk Council is tired of it. It's getting ridiculous. We're not talking about making one or two mistakes. We all do that. We're talking about serial Step and Fetchers like Jackson who don't seem to understand that their acts carry larger consequences.

If you haven't heard of Jackson, then you've missed a player who could be the next great wide receiver in football. In September

Philadelphia Eagles wide receiver DeSean Jackson runs back a 68-yard punt return and gets across the goal line for a touchdown in the second quarter of an NFL football game against the Washington Redskins on Sunday, October 5, 2008, in Philadelphia. (AP Photo/Tom Mihalek)

2008 on Monday Night Football against Dallas, a game that ended up being the most watched event in cable history, Jackson became the first NFL player in almost seven decades to open his career with two 100-yard performances. He's one of the most physically gifted young receiver in football. Unfortunately, Jackson is starting to make Terrell Owens look like Alan Greenspan.

Jackson pulled what was almost the biggest bonehead move we've seen in professional football since Leon Lett. Against a heated rival with the entire country watching, Jackson decided to showboat after making a big catch by casually tossing away the football. The problem was, he failed to first cross the goal line—and what should have been a marvelous 61-yard touchdown was negated. What was Jackson thinking? Somewhere Don Beebe was laughing his ass off again.

The Eagles still retained possession of the football and were able to score on the following play. If Philadelphia had lost that touchdown, there'd have been legitimate concern for Jackson's physical safety upon returning to Philly.

The Jerk Council can hear some black readers now. "Shut up." "You're an Uncle Tom." "All the man's doing is celebrating." No, you shut up. You're an enabler. Jackson wouldn't be one of the Jerk 100 if this was his only mistake. We all make them. Except Jackson did this in high school. The exact same thing. He was a clown in college, as well. He wants to do this. He revels in doing this. He'll likely keep doing it. There's no difference between Jackson's actions—and the cadre of fools like Owens and his ilk—and those African Americans who once debased and degraded themselves because that's what they believed whites wanted to see.

"Jackson is young and he'll learn," you respond. That might be true, but it doesn't seem like he's really interested in learning from his mistakes. He might be brainwashed into believing that's the way African Americans are supposed to behave in the workplace. No one's told him any differently. All the popular media and music do is embolden people like Jackson. He doesn't think he's doing anything wrong, and that's the most frightening part of all this.

After the football bounced back into the field of play, Jackson then did a little dance. Just beautiful. What will Jackson do next? Pull out a Sharpie? Oh wait, that's already been done.

What needs to happen is this: The Philadelphia locker room is full of great professionals, and some of those players need to constantly stay on Jackson. Then something else must occur. Some of the black players should have a chat with Jackson. They need to tell him not to become another twenty-first century sports minstrel.

It's not too late. Don't jackass yourself out of football, Mr. Action Jackson. Please.

 Nick Saban

In the summer of 2008, *Forbes Magazine* suffered from a temporary loss of blood to its normally substantial brain. The magazine named Nick Saban the most powerful coach in all of sports, forgetting how that's a serious impossibility for a college coach. Since the NFL is by far the most powerful sports league in the known galaxy, a college coach cannot be the most vital.

Saban has been called a few other things, as well: Coach Satan, Nick Satan, and Nick the Dickbag. That last one isn't very nice, even if it is a tad funny. While Saban is cherished at the University of Alabama, secure in that insular world, a king on a throne heavily protected by adoring fans, he is despised by many outside of the Alabama universe.

Saban, along with others like Bill Parcells and Bobby Petrino, represent The Weasel Coach. That's a coach who says he loves where he is and will never leave. That is, until a better job opens up—then he's gone lickety-split.

It's a disgusting two-step enacted by college coaches in particular. The college players themselves are highly restricted in their movements. Changing colleges can result in loss of scholarship or eligibility. Coaches, however, move almost at will, free from any sort of serious penalty.

Saban pulled one of the all-time great con jobs while he was coach of the Miami Dolphins. After just two seasons on the job, there were persistent rumors that Saban was leaving for Alabama. Saban was repeatedly asked about them and strongly denied their veracity. Once he even said, "I'm not going to be the Alabama coach." Some in the media actually believed Saban. It wasn't true, and Saban was soon gone.

Saban's jerkiness doesn't stop there. He once publicly used the word "coonass" and was forced to apologize. How a highly intelligent man and educator could not know the ramifications of the use of that word is stunning and frankly just plain jerky. There were more inappropriate comments. In 2007, Saban equated Alabama's embarrassing loss to Louisiana-Monroe to the devastation that were the September 11 attacks and the bombing of Pearl Harbor. Sure, comparing a game to mass murder and a horrific military attack are, of course, the same thing.

Alabama fans get extremely pissy when Saban is criticized. For now, that'll remain true. It's only a matter of time though before Saban packs his bags and leaves for another spot. It's a guarantee. It's in Saban's genome. When it happens, we'll see how the Alabama faithful respond. Maybe they'll use one of Saban's own colorful words to describe him.

Best Coaches

The Five Best Coaches in College Football History
(Weasel note from the author making a weasel explanation: This list does not include coaches from historically black colleges. Those coaches faced limited resources and extreme racism and likely did better coaching jobs than many others, but for the sake of this list, we're only mostly including major college coaches.)

5. **Alonzo Stagg** – One of the great men of innovation in sports history. He invented the presnap motion, the use of helmets, the lateral pass, and inscribing names on the back of jerseys. He also invented the huddle in the late 1800s as a way to fight crowd noise.

4. **Bear Bryant** – Won six national titles over an 18-year period. The only reason he's not rated higher is that his highly brutal practices would be practically illegal today.

3. **Glenn Scobey "Pop" Warner** – Won 318 games.

2. **Joe Paterno** – A notorious hard ass and great winner.

1. **Bobby Bowden** – This top spot might one day be owned by Pete Carroll, but for now, Bowden has it. A great combination of winner and longevity.

Eric Mangini

The Jerk Council wants to be clear about something. We don't condone Bill Belichick videotaping the coaching signals of opponents. It was wrong. It wasn't the crime of the century, but it was nevertheless wrong. Still, what Eric Mangini did was equally wrong and why he's become jerk fodder.

Mangini seems like a genuinely decent person, but that doesn't change the fact it was Mangini who likely ratted out Belichick to the NFL and the media. We use the word "likely" just for legal reasons. If you don't believe Mangini sold out Belichick, then you're one of the few people who still believe there are weapons of mass destruction in Iraq.

What makes Mangini so jerk-worthy is the degree to which he betrayed Belichick. You have to know the history between Belichick and Mangini to truly appreciate this. When Belichick coached the Cleveland Browns, he took Mangini, who was a ball boy for the club, and gave him a job assembling game and practice film. Belichick later gave Mangini an assistant's position on the staff. When Belichick went to the New York Jets, he again was good to Mangini and made him a defensive assistant.

Belichick wasn't helping Mangini completely out of the selflessness. Mangini has ability and talent; even his harshest critics will admit that. So Belichick benefited from assisting Mangini. Still, Mangini did something that's a serious violation in football, perhaps the most serious. Mangini turned on his friend. "Belichick is what he is, the New England Patriots are what they are, and Eric Mangini is what he is," wrote the Bleacher Report website. "Mangini is a traitor, a rat, a whiner, and a loser, all of the things that Bill Belichick and the Patriots organization are not." You think that's harsh? You should hear what several other coaches said about Mangini in several conversations. While many coaches in the NFL hate that Belichick cheated to the extent that he did, believe it or not, more are angry with Mangini.

Here is where Mangini gets a bit of a break. Belichick was so arrogant, videotaping right in Mangini's face, that Mangini had no choice but to rat on Belichick. Some of that is true. Maybe Mangini even privately called Belichick to warn the coach before turning on him. That is true, as well. In the end, Mangini made the decision to sell out Belichick, and he'll have to live with that decision.

Cap Anson

Cap Anson was a product of his environment. Segregation was rampant throughout American society and the sport of baseball in Anson's time from 1871–97. Yet Anson seemed to revel in this. He seemed to truly enjoy keeping African Americans out of the sport. Many people who study the history of baseball indeed credit Anson with a dubious distinction. He is considered one of the driving forces in establishing and maintaining segregation in baseball. Most people wouldn't want that on their tombstone, but it's on Anson's.

Anson was one of baseball's first superstars, and he wielded that considerable influence in several ways to keep blacks out of baseball. He declined not only to play against blacks in exhibition, but he didn't want to play anyone who even looked like they might be African American. (Not sure what Anson would've made of Vin Diesel.) One of the better examples of this happened in 1883 when Anson declined to play in an exhibition contest in Toledo, Ohio, after discovering that one of the players, a catcher named Moses Walker, was African American. Anson rethought his decision when told that if he didn't play his team would be forced to give up gate receipts. The only dark color Anson seemed to like was green.

There are other examples of Anson's bigotry, but let's not belabor the jerk point. Calling Anson a jerk actually doesn't do justice to what was a deep-seated bigotry. As the website capanson.com wrote, "It is important to remember that Cap Anson was born in Iowa in the year 1852. At that time, Iowa permitted slave ownership, and although the state sided with the Union in the Civil War, sentiment was deeply divided over the slavery issue. Anson grew up in a region where blacks were not held in high esteem. It has been said that racism is not instinctive but learned, as nature is not suicidal. It is highly likely that the seeds of Anson's personal racism were planted by the words and deeds of the white adults of his immediate surroundings."

That may be accurate, but Anson eventually became an adult, and there were millions of white Americans who knew that segregation was morally wrong and fought it. Unfortunately, Anson wasn't one of them.

82 Some Fans of the Dallas Mavericks

In July 2008, Josh Howard, a player for the Dallas Mavericks, made a comment he wishes he could take back. At a charity flag football event, a homemade video was shot of Howard disrespecting the national anthem. He was recorded saying, "The Star Spangled Banner's going on right now, and I don't celebrate that shit. I'm black." Well, whoa, big fella. You don't speak for all African Americans, my man. Who do you think you are? Martin Luther Howard?

You might feel that Howard's words and actions were anti-American, and in some ways they were. Yet what followed was equally anti-American, if not more. In fact, it was one of the more disgraceful episodes in all of sports that year.

Mark Cuban, the owner of the Mavericks, received hundreds of emails in response, and let's just say the mailers were in full redneck, jerk form. The Jerk Council is rarely shocked by the behavior of fans, but even we couldn't believe our virgin eyes and this is why we love Cuban. Besides being an excellent owner, he makes ignorant dopes accountable for their actions. He wrote in his September 2008 blog, "I wanted to thank all of you who took the time to email me with your comments on how best to deal with Josh. They were so good I thought I would share a few of them with everyone. Including the email addresses of those who were bold enough to use real email addresses. Josh realizes his comments were wrong, he understands why people are upset. He knows he has made a mistake, has apologized and will work with us. Beyond that, it's a private issue. What about the people who gave me the following advice?" Then Cuban ran many of the emails in his blog with names and IP addresses attached. It was a marvelous middle finger to Redneck Nation.

Here are two of the responses in their entirety and unedited:

> "Hi Mark, Did you know Josh Howard was an America hater when you signed him or was it a surprise? I don't spend my money on this NBA shit, I am white."
> *(Jerk logic makes absolutely no sense.)*

> "Tell Howard that him and Hussein Obama can go to another country and live if they don't want to support our symbol of freedom."
> *(Ah, the old get-out-of-the-country-if-you-don't-like-it argument.)*

Again, what Howard said was wrong, but some of the reactions to Howard's remarks were far more anti-American than anything Howard stated. And extremely jerkish.

81 Alexander Rodriguez

This is from the September 20, 2008, edition of the *New York Post*. Please, prepare yourselves.

"Alex Rodriguez wasted no time embracing single life," the paper wrote in cringe-inducing detail. "With the ink not yet dry on his divorce, the All-Star was spotted Thursday getting his blond highlights touched up at the Frederick Fekkai Salon. Wearing faded jeans and skin-tight blue T-shirt, A-Rod embraced his feminine side when stylists wrapped his head in a plastic helmet and put him under a heat lamp...Later, A-Rod asked his yes-men if 'it should be darker,' to which they responded with stunned silence."

Please. No. No. God, no. For the love of all things holy. No.

Did Jim Brown get blonde highlights? Did Babe Ruth get pedicures? Did Bill Russell shave his legs? Did Nolan Ryan get anything "touched up?" No, just no.

Imagine the thoughts of A-Rod's crew when he allegedly asked them that question—should his roots be darker? Do you think Lawrence Taylor ever turned to teammate and quarterback Phil Simms and said, "How does my hair look?"

A-Rod might end up breaking Barry Bonds' homerun record. He is perhaps the best all-around player the sport has ever seen despite his lack of production at times in the postseason. Yet

Alex Rodriguez arrives at "A Night to Benefit Raising Malawi and UNICEF" at United Nations headquarters on Wednesday, February 6, 2008, in New York with perfect hair highlights. (AP Photo/Evan Agostini)

there has always been something not quite right about A-Rod. A lack of sincerity, perhaps. A degree of phoniness, maybe. A touch of extreme arrogance, possibly. He once told *Sports Illustrated* when defending himself against criticism, "[Mike] Mussina doesn't get hammered at all. He's making a boatload of money. [Jason] Giambi's making [$20.4 million], which is fine and dandy, but it seems those guys get a pass. When people write [bad things] about me, I don't know if it's [because] I'm good-looking, I'm biracial, I make the most money, I play on the most popular team." The humility just drips off the page.

And all of this before it was proven that A-Rod is actually A-Roid. He's an admitted steroid user.

We all make mistakes, and no one is perfect. Even the Jerk Council has made a few. There's just something extremely jerky about a person who attempts to present himself one way to the public and is totally different when the media and cameras are out of range. This seems to be The Way of The Rod.

We got a glimpse of this as his extremely nasty divorce played out in the New York tabloids in 2007 and into 2008. The ugliness started when the *Post* ran a picture of A-Rod with a blonde stripper (maybe they met while both were getting their highlights done). The woman wasn't A-Rod's wife, so the tabloids were off to the races. Eventually he was linked to Madonna. Both Madonna and Rodriguez denied any hanky-panky, but neither denied they'd worked on each other's highlights.

An athlete cheating on his wife is garden-variety jerk stuff, but Rodriguez likes to present himself as Huckleberry Finn. Who, by the way, didn't have blonde highlights.

 # Babe Ruth

Maybe this is a simple case of jerk jealousy or jerk envy in the highest order. Babe Ruth became perhaps the greatest baseball star ever but did so despite being a womanizing slob who drank too much. Yes, perhaps Babe envy is rearing its ugly head because who wouldn't love to have the ability to smack home runs into another area code after a night of hard drinking and carousing with numerous women despite being married? Ah, the jerk life.

If Ruth lived today, he'd be John Daly, only not as big a loser. The blogosphere would chronicle every belch and whiskey-riddled, club-hopping escapade. Pictures of his lovers would grace the front pages of various tabloids juxtaposed with his respective wives. Ruth was extremely lucky he became great at a time when the press covered up the exploits of athletes rather than publicly discussing them. Many reporters who covered Ruth believed he had a sexually transmitted disease following Ruth's complaint of a stomachache in 1925, yet no one wrote it. When Michael Vick was sued by a woman who claimed he gave her herpes (ewwwww—allegedly), it became news across the Internet and eventually made its way into the mainstream media.

Ruth is an old-school jerk. Ruth is to jerks what the Wright brothers are to flight. Baseball historians have given the great Ruth a massive pass for his petulant behavior. It's probably a pass no baseball player has received since and never will again (see: Bonds, Barry, a.k.a. Mr. Smirk). Unless this is more of a case of the Jerk Council wishing we could excel and get babes while doing nothing but drinking and stuffing our faces.

79 Eugene Robinson

On the morning of Super Bowl XXXIII in Miami my cell phone rang. There was a panicked voice on the other line. It was one of the players for the Atlanta Falcons I had known for some time. The Falcons were just hours away from playing the Denver Broncos in the biggest football game in the world.

"We're fucked," were the first words the player said.

"What?" I responded.

"We are absolutely fucking fucked," the player said. "We're fucked."

I think he believed they were (expletive).

"Eugene threw away the Super Bowl to get his dick sucked," the player said.

"What the hell are you talking about?"

He proceeded to tell me that star Atlanta defensive back Eugene Robinson had been arrested by undercover police officers for soliciting a prostitute. The details of the arrest soon emerged. Robinson had offered a female officer $40 for oral sex the night before the Super Bowl in February 1999 and was busted.

In the pantheon of jerks, Robinson seems like the least likely candidate. Having interviewed Robinson several times, he is one of the nicest, likeable, and intelligent athletes the Jerk Council has ever come across. He was highly respected by almost everyone around him.

Robinson nevertheless enters definite jerk territory because of what he did the night before the Super Bowl. The morning before the game, Robinson had accepted an award from the Christian-based organization Athletes in Action. He was named the group's Bart Starr Award winner—given to the player with high moral character. For years, Robinson had preached about his faith in God and his dedication to family. He was a devout Christian—except for the attempted blowjob from a prostitute part—other than that, he was perfect Christian material.

Robinson isn't your classic jerk, but he is your stereotypical hypocrite and that makes him perfect jerk material.

Robinson's teammate who phoned the day of the Super Bowl remained furious with Robinson for years. So did other Falcons players. My player friend once asked, "What would you rather have, a blowjob or a Super Bowl ring? The answer is clear." Hmmm...oral sex or a Super Bowl? Super Bowl or oral sex? The answer isn't so clear, dude. Let's think on that one.

After dozens of interviews with players across the NFL, I would later discover that it's not unusual for athletes to use the services of prostitutes the night before big games as a way to relieve stress.

Haven't these players ever heard of yoga?

Robinson's pre–Super Bowl attempt to snag glorious hooker love would backfire on the field as well as off of it. Robinson blew a pass coverage that led to an 80-yard Denver touchdown. Later in the game, he missed a key tackle. It is, without question, one of the most embarrassing public moments an athlete has ever experienced.

Robinson was shell-shocked and apologetic after the game. The damage, however, was done. He played a few more seasons in the NFL before retiring. Robinson became a football coach at a high school in North Carolina where presumably school officials keep the prostitutes as far away from campus as possible.

 # Uga V

The Jerk Council loves dogs: fuzzy ones, fat ones, skinny ones, tall ones, dogs that bark, dogs that eat peanut butter and cheese. All dogs, all the time, so it pains us to name our first four-legged jerk: Uga V.

Uga V is part of a long tradition of fine mascots for the Georgia Bulldogs who have represented their football team with great slobbering distinction. That is until Uga V committed attempted third-degree assault on the cajones of an Auburn football player.

The scene of the crime was the Georgia end zone in a 1995 game against Auburn. Robert Baker, the wide receiver for the Tigers, scored on a 21-yard touchdown pass. Soon after the catch, Uga V lunged for Baker, snapping at his midsection, which is a polite way to say Baker almost had an involuntary castration.

What the hell? Who trained Uga V? Michael Vick?

A photographer captured the entire incident, and Uga V became a national sensation. During the game, analyst Sean McDonough crooned, "The Georgia defense might want to consider dressing Uga." Sorry Sean, but we here at the Jerk Council don't condone unsportsmanlike conduct at worst and penile mutilation at best. No one should ever, ever look lightly on dog-on-crotch attacks.

Sadly, since that infamous moment, Uga V has departed for the doghouse in the sky, thankfully minus Baker's genitals. Georgia remains highly proud of its pooch's legacy, and certainly Uga V did perform a great deal of good while alive and it wasn't just sniffing the rear ends of other dogs. He was a great warrior who defended his turf and won the honor of being the first dog jerk in jerk history. What more could Uga V ask for?

The Greatest Mascot Fight Ever

It isn't Uga V vs. Robert Baker, otherwise known as "The Thrilla' with the Uga." It's a classic mascot brawl, truly the best ever. It featured the Oregon Duck against the Houston Cougar in a 2007 game between the two schools. It started out as playful, but then the Oregon Duck went ballistic and an all-out brawl ensued. The Cougar was getting his fuzzy butt beat so badly that the Houston cheerleaders had to pull the Duck off of him. Incredibly, the Oregon mascot was suspended for one game. Nothing like roasted duck on the menu.

Bill Belichick

We have always liked Bill Belichick. We believe that he is the best coach professional football has ever seen. That's not exaggeration or hyperbole. He won multiple Super Bowls in a dramatically short period of time. As a defensive coordinator for the New York Giants, he developed and enacted game plans that frustrated and limited opponents. Belichick's gotten the most out of players in an age when athletes view authority figures with the same disdain that scientists view the Andromeda Strain. He might also be the most intelligent coach we've seen. He's better than Lombardi or Shula or Noll. Go ahead and argue. Go ahead and throw this book against the wall in frustration (just don't burn it). Call us the biggest dumbasses in history, but our position is easily defensible.

Defending the architect of the spy case heard around the Milky Way Galaxy is not so easy, however. You can say that coaches have videotaped and stolen signals from other teams for decades, if not since the modern beginnings of the sport. You can mention quotes like this from former Dallas Cowboys coach Jimmy Johnson who said on Fox Sports, "This is exactly how I was told to do it eighteen years ago by a Kansas City Chiefs scout. I tried it, but I didn't think it helped us. Bill Belichick was wrong because he videotaped signals after a memo was sent out to all of the teams saying not to do it. But what irritates me is hearing some reactions from players and coaches. These players don't know what their coaches are doing. And some of the coaches have selective amnesia, because I know for a fact there were various teams doing this. That's why the memo was sent to everybody. That doesn't make [Belichick] right, but a lot of teams are doing this."

No one wants to hear these rationales, and if it sounds like the normally snippety Jerk Council is offering a defense of Belichick, well, we are. Sort of. This is not to defend his actions; they were wrong, thus his position on this jerk list. But Belichick's acts also should not be seen in a vacuum. There are numerous other NFL videographers who have and still are taping signals. It's just that Belichick was the one who got caught.

76 Randy Moss

In January 2005, one of the more confounding athletes in recent history scored a touchdown during a playoff game at Green Bay's famous Lambeau Field. He was a Minnesota Viking and not a Packer, so he didn't do the Lambeau Leap. Instead, Randy Moss did something rather odd. He simulated pulling his pants down and going to the bathroom. For those who didn't see it, Moss wasn't simulating doing a No. 1—it was the No. 2 (suddenly we feel like we're four years old).

Frankly, what Moss did was just nasty. Imagine sitting at home and watching the game with your kids or having a little jerk chicken for dinner, and suddenly some dude imitating taking a poo pops up on your screen. It doesn't matter that Moss was getting revenge on Packers fans that often moon the team buses of opponents as they enter the stadium. It was a jerk move.

Minnesota Vikings receiver Randy Moss bends over to the crowd and makes rude gestures after catching a 34-yard touchdown pass in the fourth quarter of the Vikings' NFC wild card game against the Green Bay Packers on January 9, 2005, in Green Bay, Wisconsin.

The Council doesn't mind post-touchdown celebrations or sack dances. We're not all up in arms if someone shakes their booty as long as they're creative and not poor sports. We're known to shake our ass after writing a good paragraph or two. Moss crossed the line, however. Then again, Moss often crosses the line. In a 2005 interview with HBO's Bryant Gumbel, Moss admitted to occasional marijuana use during his NFL career. Who admits that on national television?

What truly makes Moss jerk-worthy is how he's failed to consistently maximize his eye-popping ability. Moss is occasionally flat-out lazy and uninspired. When he was with the Oakland Raiders, he was at times an utter disgrace, jogging through routes when the football wasn't coming his way or refusing to block. Moss is a front-runner—brilliant when the offense runs smoothly and lackadaisical when it doesn't. If there is a classic jerk trademark, it's a lack of effort, and lack of effort frustrates sports fans almost more than anything else.

Benny Silman

A great scandal came to an official end in 1998 when Robert Broomfield, a U.S. District Court judge, handed down what was an extreme but probably deserved sentence to Benny Silman. Broomfield gave Silman a 42-month sentence for fixing basketball games during the 1994 Arizona State season when Silman was a student looking to make some quick cash. Silman did make the money he was looking for, but in the process he ended up in sports infamy as well as the prison system. "The gambling here went beyond just yourself," Broomfield told Silman, according to the Associated Press, "it affects a lot of us."

In many ways the sports world owes Silman. What happened at Arizona State was a reminder of how vulnerable some high-profile sports remain to game-fixers. The Black Sox scandal apparently wasn't enough of a cautionary tale.

Silman bribed two Sun Devil players to miss shots in several different games so dirt bag gamblers could beat the spread. At the sentencing, Silman blamed his gambling on alcohol and drug abuse, but it's likely that his ego was greatly involved. Silman controlled the outcome of a handful of games, and in a strange

> ### Hard-Working Athletes
> *The Five Hardest-Working Athletes in Sports Today*
>
> **5. Michael Phelps –** Win as many gold medals as Phelps and you must be an incredibly hard worker, pot-smoking aside.
>
> **4. Hines Ward –** Best blocking wide receiver in football.
>
> **3. Tiger Woods –** Possesses more than great natural ability.
>
> **2. Terrell Owens –** A jerk but a hard-working jerk.
>
> **I. Lance Armstrong –** A workout freak who hopefully has never been juiced.

way, it allowed him to see into the future. He knew something others didn't. He knew who'd win. That kind of power and knowledge is something no one should ever possess. Silman was lucky he was sentenced to only 42 months in prison. If it were up to us it would have been a lot longer.

Athletes Who Thank God

The Jerk Council does not want to offend God. That would be bad. We do not desire God sending plagues or pestilence our way, nor do we want anything to do with Satan or hellfire or pitchforks. So we'll leave the God jokes to Bill Maher, thank you very much.

But perhaps the most singularly annoying and jerky thing in sports are athletes thanking God. Thank you God for our win.

Thank you Lord for my three touchdowns. Thank you God for the other team missing the game-winning basket. Thank you, thank you, and thank you. God obviously cares about sports. Why else would She create nachos and TiVo? Yet the age-old argument stands—doesn't God have bigger things to worry about than sports? It's a very fair question.

It's extraordinarily egotistical and self-centered to think God cares about something that in the grand scheme of the universe means very little. It's one thing to ask God not to get injured in a sporting event; it's another to think God cares about who wins or loses.

What Dallas safety Roy Williams stated in June 2008 was even more ridiculous. Williams compared being attacked by critics for his poor play to the persecution of Jesus. "Ever since I've rededicated my life to Christ, I've caught way more persecution now," he told the *Oklahoman* newspaper. "But it's a beautiful thing because I know it's a breakthrough coming for me. I welcome it. What makes me any better than Christ? He was persecuted and I've been persecuted. My teammates know where my heart is. They know where my mind is at." As CBSSports.com, national columnist Gregg Doyel wrote: "Williams' heart may be in the right place, but his brain needs work if it sees parallels between the persecution of Jesus and the persecution of a $25 million safety. Beaten by Roman soldiers, beaten by Randy Moss—what's the difference?"

Again, this isn't to mock anyone's faith, but some of this has just gotten insane. Now, excuse the Jerk Council while we take cover from the lightning that's about to strike us.

> ## Don't Thank God
> ### Three Things Athletes Should Not Thank God For
>
> **3. Touchdowns —** They're too common for God to care about, that is, unless you're the Oakland Raiders, in which case you should pray once an hour.
>
> **2. First downs —** Ditto.
>
> **1. Victories —** God's far too preoccupied with Michael Jackson to care about wins and losses.

Lawrence Phillips

Lawrence Phillips was first a thug. Then he was a bust. Then he was a thug again. Then a bust again. Now he's simply a jerk incarnate.

Phillips is a jerk rarity. He turned out to be a horrible NFL player, despite pro football scouts swearing he'd be the next Jim Brown, he had an awful attitude, a poor work ethic, and he was a woman beater. Perfect. If there were a Mt. Rushmore of jerks, Phillips would barely miss being on it.

His career as a woman beater started early when he dragged a girlfriend, a fellow University of Nebraska athlete, down a flight of stairs by her hair. Phillips = Stone Age. Coach Tom Osborne, always the molder of men, only suspended Phillips for his horrid act instead of kicking him off the team. Phillips wouldn't learn his lesson. After his spectacular Nebraska career, years later, he faced several more accusations of violence against women, including one where an ex-girlfriend accused Phillips of choking her to the point where she became unconscious.

Phillips was also accused in 2005 of driving his car into a group of teenagers after they argued over calls in a pick-up basketball game in California. Well, that we can understand. Who hasn't wanted to run over some loud-mouth punk who constantly talked smack during a pick-up game?

Phillips was the sixth overall draft pick in 1996 by the St. Louis Rams despite his troubled Nebraska career—again demonstrating that NFL teams would draft Saddam Hussein if he ran a 4.4-second 40-yard dash. Phillips lived up to the challenge by getting cut just a short time later after he refused to practice following a hissy fit with St. Louis coach Dick Vermeil.

There have been few combinations of bust and jerk better than Phillips. Indeed, there may never be another one like him— and that's a good thing.

Some Chicago Cubs Fans

"Hey Mike, if I ever see you crossing the street, I'm going to run over your black ass with my car."

A FLORIDA GATOR FAN IN AN EMAIL TO ME.
I'M CAREFUL NOT TO JAYWALK NOW.

"I think I speak for the city of Louisville when I say I hope you get cancer and die."

—A CARDINALS FAN TO ME, AND SORRY DUDE,
MY HEALTH IS GREAT.

"I wish your mom had an abortion when she was pregnant with you."
—A NASCAR FAN. SOMETIMES SO DOES MY MOM.

"I'm coming over to bomb your house. I hope your ugly dog is in it when I do."
—A GATOR FAN TO ME. MY DOG DISARMS BOMBS, BY THE WAY.

"You're a douche bag. And you're fucking ugly. You're a fucking ugly douche bag."
—AN OHIO STATE FAN TO ME AND ONE OF MY FAVORITE PIECES OF MAIL EVER.

"I hate you, you dickhead. You make me sick. But I can't stop reading you, asshole."
—A GATOR FAN. AH...THANKS. I THINK.

Those are letters and emails I recently received from readers, and I'm just an opinionated sports journalist. Imagine the reaction to this man.

It is October 2003 and a shy, passionate fan of the Chicago Cubs sitting in Aisle 4, Row 8, and Seat 113 at Wrigley Field does something that almost any human being would: he instinctively reaches for a foul ball that suddenly appears within his grasp.

Steve Bartman had no idea that such a simple, innocent act would lead to the near destruction of his life thanks to a weapons-grade campaign of insults, cyber-stalking, and belligerence from fans of the Cubs that would last for years.

What happened to Bartman is one of the better examples of why some sports fans are not just jerks but flat-out losers and why often the media's behavior can be just as petulant as the jerk fans themselves.

The ball Bartman interfered with likely wasn't going to be caught by outfielder Moises Alou. That didn't matter. Nor did the

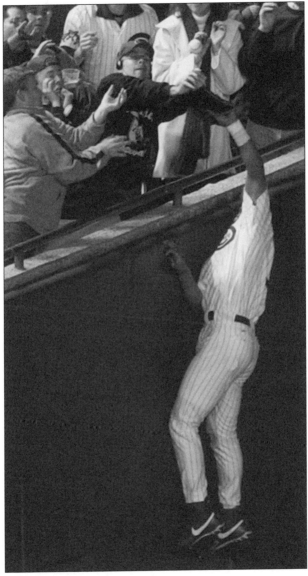

Chicago Cubs left fielder Moises Alou reaches into the stands for a foul ball tipped by fan Steve Bartman in the eighth inning during Game 6 of the National League Championship Series on October 14, 2003, at Wrigley Field in Chicago. Poor Steve Bartman.

fact that the entire Cubs team unraveled in that Game 6 thanks to a series of blunders and an eight-run inning. Not to mention that the Cubs still had a chance to win the series in Game 7 and beat the Florida Marlins. None of that mattered to Cubs fans. They focused their ire on Bartman and his reaching for a ball that wouldn't have been caught.

What happened next was simply incredible, unbelievable, and unforgivable. Bartman, his head feebly protected by a jacket, was pummeled with beer and obscenities by fans. He would receive death threats at his place of business. *Death threats.* Hundreds of them. Police were called in to protect his home. There were Internet hoaxes linking Bartman to the September 11th attacks. When Bartman understandably went into seclusion, newspaper cartoonists sarcastically showed Bartman hiding in a darkened cave with Hussein and Osama bin Laden. Chicago columnist Jay Mariotti would later apologize for the harsh columns he wrote about Bartman. Even the former governor of Illinois, named Rod Blagojevich, got into the Bartman bashing act by saying Bartman had "better join the witness protection program."

Cubs fans were relentless and brutal. The threats against Bartman would continue for years. That night, thousands of Cubs fans yelled, in unison, "Kill him!"

To this day, Bartman refuses to enter the public eye. He has hired a PR person to field inquiries from the media, and that person says Bartman still wants to remain in the backdrop. Can't blame Bartman, can you? There is little question that if Bartman went to Wrigley Field and was identified by fans, his physical safety might be in question.

Sports fans engaging in violent threatening behavior, unfortunately, is not unusual (I've received death threats from Florida Gator fans). With Bartman, however, you saw the great extreme of human nature and fandom—and jerkdom. The psychology of Cubs fans is interesting in the Bartman case. They searched for someone to blame for the Cubs losing to the Marlins, and instead of focusing on the players, they took out their wrath on a lone fan. It was classic mob mentality.

It could be years before Bartman can safely attend another Cubs game with everyone in the stadium knowing he is there. In fact, it may never happen.

71 Elijah Dukes

We don't want to make you all depressed with a jerk here and a jerk there. Drug guy behind this corner, woman beater behind the other, John Daly busy getting divorced for the fifteenth time and eating too many bearclaws. Yet part of this book is an educational process. Getting educated about jerks in turn prevents you from becoming one. We also don't want any jerks illegally crossing our borders and making Lou Dobbs angry. That's our public service bit for queen and country.

The pointing out of jerks, however, cannot be helped. The sports world at times is simply overflowing with them. It's incredible, actually. Take the alleged unbridled arrogance and frightening meanness of one Major League Baseball player, Elijah Dukes. In 2007, his wife was teaching in a middle school classroom when Dukes, according to court filings, angrily stormed into the room and demanded to speak with her. He was later banned from the school, and she sought a restraining order against him.

Dukes' alleged horrific harassment of his wife didn't stop there. She claimed Dukes threatened to kill her and sent a photo of a handgun to her cell phone. The *St. Petersburg Times* newspaper quoted Dukes as saying on a phone message to his wife, "You dead, dawg. I ain't even bulls---. Your kids, too."

This is what's objectionable: It's not just Dukes himself. If these accusations are true—and there's little doubt they are—he should be sent to prison, and he's lucky he's not there at this very moment. He's a turd. We know this. The larger problem remains the teams and colleges that employ these vicious jerks. There are mistakes and then there are horrific mistakes. Teams need to ban players like Lawrence Phillips and Dukes the first time they physically harm or threaten a wife or girlfriend. Those are the rules most people in workplaces outside of professional sports live by. If you ever threatened to kill your wife or her kids and your employer discovered this fact, you'd be fired. There'd likely be no warning. There'd be no second chance. You'd be gone.

Why isn't it the same for athletes like Dukes?

Uday Hussein

This entrant raises an interesting question we'll be forced to deal with later in this jerk novella: can a murderer and torturer be a jerk?

Jerks are garden variety, well, jerks. Hussein was a killer and rapist. Breaking news here—it's worse to be a murderer than a jerk. Yet for the sake of this particular jerk (and later with our top two jerks), jerk/murderers shall occasionally be interchanged. This is Commandment One in the Jerk Manifesto.

Few people embody the jerk/murderer persona better than Uday Hussein. For decades, Hussein ran Iraq's Olympic Committee and its soccer program with the proverbial iron hand. It's believed Hussein killed dozens of athletes who failed to win in international competitions and tortured others. An anonymous State Department official told *Sports Illustrated*, "Two stories about Uday leap to mind. The first is the caning of the feet—called falaka—of the soccer team. That form of torture [was] well known to be used by Saddam's forces as well. They beat the soles of the feet, which breaks a lot of the smaller bones, causes massive swelling, and leaves victims unable to walk for a while. There were also reports that after a loss Uday forced the volleyball team, which was made up of taller athletes, to remain in a room he had constructed with a five-foot-high ceiling. He built the room so small that not all of them could sit at the same time. The only way they could fit was by having half of them standing and leaning over while the other half were sitting with their knees in their chests. He considered this a motivational technique. There was always a psychological element to the kind of torture Uday employed. You are supposed to play like tall players, so feel what it is like to be small. For the soccer players, you are supposed to be fast and quick, so I am going to beat your feet and ruin your livelihood. That was his thinking."

That quote just about says it all.

In 2008, with Uday dead following the second Iraq War, Iraqi soccer players experienced a new sense of freedom. The torturer was gone, and the team was actually cleared to qualify in the 2010 World Cup.

Rick Dutrow Jr.

There are things to admire about Rick Dutrow, Jr. He overcame a horrific tragedy, the murder of his girlfriend, years ago. He beat drug abuse, and before becoming a Derby winner, he was actually homeless, sleeping in a barn, because his business had failed so badly. Those things make him un-jerk-worthy.

This is what makes him jerk-worthy. His horse, Big Brown, won the Kentucky Derby and Preakness in 2008. The Belmont was a chance for Triple Crown greatness, but Big Brown failed

Big Brown's jockey Kent Desormeaux tries to keep the Triple Crown hopeful under control as he crosses the finish line last in the 140th Belmont Stakes at Belmont Park in Elmont, New York, on Saturday, June 7, 2008. (AP Photo/Rob Carr)

and Dutrow did something absolutely unforgivable—he publicly blamed the jockey for the loss. "Big Brown is a horse," wrote CBSSports.com columnist Gregg Doyel. "Dutrow is a horse's ass."

Dutrow spoke about jockey Kent Desormeaux after the race like his name was Clark Kent, when in fact Brown's rider is a Hall of Famer with more than two decades of experience. Before the race, Dutrow was almost worse in his behavior than after it. He bragged to reporters about how Big Brown was practically unstoppable. "I am trying to be humble," Dutrow told reporters. "These horses cannot run with Big Brown." He added that the Triple Crown was "a foregone conclusion."

In the end, Dutrow threw his jockey under the bus, er, hooves. It was petulant and unnecessary particularly since it wasn't the fault of Desormeaux. Dutrow is a perfect example of how hubris can get out of control. He tasted success and let it go completely to his head by targeting a great jockey without discretion or sympathy.

68 Travis Henry

Two things you never want to see in the same sentence with your name: the words "multi-kilogram cocaine transaction" and the phrase "fathered nine children by nine different women located in four states."

Travis Henry, you old dog, you.

You know things are bad when detention by police in 2008 for alleged cocaine dealing isn't the most embarrassing thing about being Travis Henry. No, Henry became well known around the country for something else. A child paternity lawsuit showed that Henry had nine children by nine different women across four different states. Henry's sperm does so much traveling it should earn frequent flier miles.

Those are two quite jerkish things. If there's one thing we hate here, it's drug dealers and the waste of good ovaries. Truly pathetic, however, is that according to court documents, Henry was ordered to pay child support but on many occasions didn't, claiming he was broke. Yet Henry, those documents state, had a $100,000 car and spent $146,000 on jewelry. So he could allegedly afford fancy cars and plenty of bling, but he had to be forced to provide for his children.

It's an awful phenomenon. Players like former Major League Baseball great Steve Garvey and perhaps the poster boy for alleged irresponsible athlete dads, former NBA player Shawn Kemp, and many others earn significant salaries and buy expensive things but cannot raise their children. It's terribly irresponsible on numerous levels.

Henry maintained he was a responsible father but the court documents and testimony state otherwise. It's a shame. The anger you feel at players like Henry is only matched by the sympathy you have for kids who end up not having their fathers around.

67 China

This from a lead in *Time* magazine about China's disposable athletes: "When Zou Chunlan left school to become a professional athlete, her recruiting coach assured the

13-year-old that the nation's huge sports bureaucracy would look after her for the rest of her life. All she had to worry about was winning. For a decade, Zou followed his advice, winning the 48-kg national weightlifting title in 1990 when she was 19-years-old and pocketing four other national championships. But when she retired in 1993, Zou discovered that the coach's side of the bargain wasn't going to be met. After three years of menial jobs in the women's weightlifting team's kitchen, she was asked to leave."

As *Time* also reported, because she was asked—forced, basically—to invest so much time into her athletic life, she was able to get very little formal education. In America, many times, when an Olympian's career is over, there are endorsement deals, or they can return to school. Not so in China. Zou was basically forced into a life of menial labor. She sold lamb kebabs on street corners and worked on construction sites. She ended up working as a masseuse in a bathhouse.

"Zou's national medals are worthless," a weightlifting coach told the *Beijing News*. "There are world champions who end up jobless after retirement."

This isn't to say American athletes don't suffer similar fates—the NFL has been known to ignore its seriously debilitated players after they retire—but China is notorious for taking extremely young athletes, wringing every ounce of athletic ability out of them like a dishrag, then dumping them when their careers are through. Again, this isn't a phenomenon unique to China, but that country seems to excel at it and possibly even take pride in it.

The *China Sports Daily* reported in 2007 that some 80 percent of China's 300,000 ex-athletes continue to struggle with joblessness, poverty, or injury. Zou departed her sport with a truly personal and embarrassing legacy. She was told to take what her coach called "nutrition pills." The pills were in fact steroids, and they caused her to grow a beard that she needs to shave daily. The performance enhancers also made Zou infertile.

China has long legacies of human rights abuses and what happens to ex-athletes might not compare to what happens to people in Tibet, but what China is doing to its own athletic young is still deeply disturbing. "I gave my youth to sport," Zou told *Time*, "but in return, I was thrown out like garbage with no knowledge, no skill, and a barren womb."

It's rare that an entire country is named a jerk, but in the case of China, it's a well-earned title.

The Other Vick

There are entire countries like China that are jerkish, and then are actually Jerk Brothers. Or to borrow a duo from the 1980s, there are the Jerky Boys. They would be the Vicks. You know all about Mike "The Dog Whisperer" Vick, but his younger brother Marcus is also familiar with the soft and cuddly feeling of handcuffs. While Marcus was no world-class screw-up like his older bro', he still made his way into the legal system. In some ways, Marcus was a faster and stronger Michael, yet like his older brother, he fell in love with guns and ganja. Marcus played at Virginia Tech—like Michael—but was suspended for an entire season after a marijuana possession rap and accusations that he was involved with a female minor.

It's stunning, actually, how similar the downfalls of the two brothers were. Michael faced accusations about marijuana use, and so did Marcus. Michael once gave the middle finger to a

Virginia Tech quarterback Marcus Vick, left, and his attorney, Lawrence H. Woodward, second from left, leave the New Kent County Courthouse on Tuesday, August 3, 2004, in New Kent, Virginia. Vick pleaded guilty to reckless driving and no contest to marijuana possession shortly after he was suspended from the university for the 2004 season. (AP Photo/Richmond Times-Dispatch, P. Kevin Morley)

crowd of fans, and so did Marcus, who committed his single-digit act of rebellion at West Virginia. Not to be outdone, Marcus added to his on-field shenanigans when, for practically no reason, he stomped the leg of a University of Louisville player during a bowl game. It was an ugly act that led to Marcus' dismissal from Virginia Tech.

Marcus wasn't done. In another case of NFL teams doing anything for talent (teams would draft Rachel Ray, if she could bench press 350 lbs.), Marcus was signed by the Miami Dolphins.

There he proceeded to proudly carry the Vick name. A small group of customers at a McDonald's in Virginia claimed Marcus pulled a gun on them. He eventually pled guilty to disorderly conduct. The event was humorously documented in all its Photo Shopped glory by the website Deadspin.com, which put guns in Vick's hand and had him standing outside of a McDonald's.

Even the NFL, which will sign anyone, had had it with Marcus. He was gone in a short time from the Dolphins.

The problem with Marcus and Michael is not just the waste of talent but the lack of appreciation for what they had. This isn't to mean they should be grateful to the college and the NFL. Colleges exploit many of these players, and NFL teams make truckloads of money off of them. It's a highly symbiotic process. There are still some players who just don't get it, though. Sports provide opportunities for athletes to reinvent their lives, take care of family members, and use their platform to perhaps better society. Sounds corny, but look at athletes like Jackie Robinson, Muhammad Ali, Jim Brown, and Warrick Dunn, among many others. They used their profession as currency or a platform—maybe the proper phrase is a launching pad—to achieve bigger and better things even if the initial goal was to simply make money and secure their future. Instead, players like Marcus smoke away their futures. Again, we all make mistakes, but it's the serial quality of mistakes that is both maddening and saddening.

Despite numerous mishaps and opportunities to learn from his mistakes, Marcus hasn't. In the spring of 2008, Marcus was stopped by police and charged with driving under the influence as well as driving on a suspended license, reckless driving, and the misdemeanor charge of eluding police. The latest trouble means Marcus will never play football again unless it's for the Mean Machine.

Underachievers

Five Biggest Underachievers,
otherwise known as the All-Crash Team.

5. **Ryan Leaf** – A top draft pick who became more famous for screaming at a reporter than playing football.

4. **Isaiah Rider** – Pegged as the next Michael Jordan, which is tremendously unfair. You could see him literally crumble under the weight of those impossible expectations.

3. **Derrick Coleman** – Never lived up to lofty expectations.

2. **Sonny Liston** – One of the most overrated fighters in history.

1. **Tony Mandarich** – Graced the cover of *Sports Illustrated* and hailed as the next great offensive lineman. It never happened.

Ty Cobb

One of the more talented writers of all time, the late Shirley Povich of the *Washington Post*, produced one of the greatest takedowns ever about a professional athlete. The subject was Ty Cobb. Wrote Povich in 1995: "Ty Cobb was, indeed, a vicious, demonic fiend who took to the ballfield every day with blood—not his own—in his eye. And how he cut and ravaged and savaged his way to all those records (90) he put in baseball's archives. Yes, the greatest player of all time was baseball's preeminent unconscionable scoundrel; as miserable a cretin as ever pulled on a uniform, and an outspoken racial bigot to boot. Cobb not only honed his spikes to his desired cutting edge for any infielders who got in his way, but off the field he was often an instant heel who beat up on waiters and bartenders and any civilians he conjectured as unfriendly, including any in the grandstands."

How'd Mr. Povich really feel?

Cobb was easily the meanest man to ever play the sport. He made Barry Bonds look like a Buddhist monk. The worst part about Cobb is that he seemed to relish his jerkdom. Some jerks end up stuck in jerky circumstances that aren't entirely the fault of their own. Cobb was different. He liked inflicting injury—physical or verbal—on almost anyone and everyone, on the baseball diamond or off of it. In 1907, Cobb got into a fistfight with a groundskeeper because of his unhappiness with

---

Baseball's Best Ever
Top Five Baseball Players of All Time

5. Sidd Finch – Just kidding.

5. Lou Gehrig – His consecutive-game streak stood for decades.

4. Hank Aaron – A great hitter who produced despite numerous death threats as he approached Ruth's record.

3. Ty Cobb – Great hitter and scoundrel.

2. Willie Mays – The best all-around player baseball has ever seen.

1. Babe Ruth – Not certain if he's the eternal talent many baseball historians claim. His lack of athleticism would not translate well in today's baseball. But his production was almost surreal.

the condition of the playing field. Then he ended up choking the man's wife when she tried to stop Cobb. He attacked a heckler in the stands. He was jealous of Babe Ruth.

Again, despite his undeniable talent as a player, Cobb truly seemed to enjoy being vicious. Despicable is a hard word, and while the Jerk Council always tries to keep its sense of humor, it's difficult to do so when discussing Cobb. Cobb is fascinating in that he brought so much beauty and grace to the sport while also sabotaging it with his unapologetic brutality.

Jayson Williams, former player for the New Jersey Nets

The case of Williams is one of guns and arrogance, arrogance and more guns. Now, before you gun crazies fire off emails to the publisher, let's get this straight: the Jerk Council is not anti-gun. We're ex-military—former Army, thank you very much—and love to target shoot. Not kill things. Target shoot…at paper targets. Since we're horrible shots, we love to use a target of John Daly's ass—nice and huge. You don't need Lasik surgery to hit that big old thing.

Still, there is something just insane about owning the kind of firepower Williams did before he shot and killed an innocent human being, limousine driver Gus Christofi, and was then accused of trying to cover up the killing. The killing took place in Williams' home where according to court testimony he kept four 12-gauge shotguns and a powerful 30-06 rifle. Most of the weapons were kept in a gun cabinet and were loaded.

This is something we just don't understand. Why does a civilian need four shotguns? Four? What's the point? Williams lived in New Jersey, not Afghanistan. He didn't live in a tough part of Jersey, either. He lived in a 65-room mansion that contained a barn holding 450 animals. In other words, Williams wasn't struggling.

You keep that many loaded weapons on the premises and it seems only a matter of time before a tragedy occurs like the one that led to Christofi's death. Williams was playing with one of them when it discharged. He was accused of wiping the gun down so his fingerprints wouldn't be found on it. He was acquitted on many of the serious charges, but a jury deadlocked on the charge of reckless manslaughter. He faces a retrial on that and other alleged crimes.

That case wasn't the first where Williams was careless with a gun. In his autobiography, Williams wrote that while he and former New York Jets wide receiver Wayne Chrebet, a friend of Williams, were on a skeet-shooting range, Williams almost accidentally shot Chrebet.

Athletes have long had a fascination with guns. Former Detroit Lions player Lomas Brown, always one of the classiest players in football during his 19 years in the NFL, told the *New York Times* in 2003, "I think the vast majority of players in the NFL have guns," said Brown. "Just about every guy I played with in the NFL had a gun. Almost every player I knew had one. Guns are rampant in football. You have all these players packing guns wherever they go. It's a disaster waiting to happen."

That's just one sport. It's probably similar in others, if not the majority of them. There are too many athletes, we believe, not to mention people in general, who purchase guns but don't have the suitable training on how to use them or the proper temperament, either. Williams learned his lesson about just how deadly a gun can be in the hands of a careless man. Unfortunately, it took someone's death to absorb that lesson.

Chris Henry

This is how low Chris Henry had sunk in 2008. Henry phoned former Dallas Cowboys wide-receiver-turned-radio-host Michael Irvin for help in cleaning up his act. Now, we like Irvin. At heart a good dude, but Henry calling Irvin for advice on how to stay out of trouble is like a drug addict phoning Robert Downey Jr. for counsel on how to avoid cocaine use. It makes no sense. You wouldn't ask George Bush for advice on pronouncing "nuclear" would you?

To say that Henry's been a disaster is an understatement. Rather than doing the usual bomb-throwing from our jerk-reinforced bunker, we're just going to list Henry's transgressions and let you assign your own DefCon jerk score. The following information is gathered from various news sources including the *Cincinnati Enquirer* and the *Ohio Penal System Gazette*. Okay that last one is a joke but not so far off.

College: Suspended for one game because of behavioral issues. *Henry was just getting started, folks.*

2005: Police find marijuana in Henry's shoes during a traffic stop after Henry was pulled over for speeding. *Is that where dope fiends hide their stash? In their shoes? Isn't that...disgusting? Doesn't the pot smell like feet after you start smoking it? Then again, pot sort of smells like feet anyway. Well, so we're told.*

2006: Arrest for multiple gun charges and aggravated assault. *Guns and NFL players.*

Cincinnati Bengals wide receiver Chris Henry, left, stands with his attorney Perry Ancona, right, in Hamilton County Municipal Court during his arraignment Thursday, April 3, 2008, in Cincinnati. The Bengals released Henry shortly before he pleaded not guilty to charges of assault and criminal damaging. (AP Photo/David Kohl)

2006: Caught drunk driving. *Then phoned Robert Downey Jr. for advice.*

2006: Suspended by the NFL for violating various policies.

2007: Suspended for the first eight games of the season. *Of course, he used the time to reflect on his life, to seek help, and to try and better himself and make the world a better place.*

2007: Pled guilty to providing alcohol to minors. *Or not.*

There's more, but this book is only supposed to be a few hundred pages. If we detailed his entire record, this book would be thicker than seven Bibles.

Henry has done something that's rare in the NFL. Among most fans, even Bengals fans, he's inspired both bewilderment at the numerous chances given to him by the Bengals and unequivocal, universal disgust.

It was thought that after his last bout with the legal system that Henry would never play football again, but the Bengals welcomed Henry back with open handcuffs, ah, arms.

That wasn't a shock. As we've stated before—and it's a main theme—teams will do anything for talent. Anything. Even put up with a punk like Henry.

62 Evander Holyfield

There are hardcore jerks like Henry and John Daly, and then there are mystifying jerks like Evander Holyfield.

Just…absolutely…mind-boggling.

Holyfield is one of the greatest boxing champions ever and at one point one of the richest. Holyfield has grossed $248 million in ring purses. No, your eyes did not misread. That's $248 million. Do you know how many strippers that could get? Excuse us, we meant, do you know how many starving children that could feed?

At one point, according to various published reports, including the *Atlanta Journal-Constitution,* during a six-fight stretch from 1996 through 1998, he earned a staggering $107 million.

Now it's just about gone, spent on exorbitant homes and costly divorces. All that money down the drain. Holyfield is so broke he puts his paper plates in the dishwasher. That is, if he had a dishwasher.

In 1997, as the *AJC* and other news media reported, he owned a house that cost a stunning $1.2 million a year to run because of extensive water and power usage, as well as lawn care. Damn, dude, trim the hedges yourself and save thousands of dollars.

Or better yet, pay us to do it. We'll only charge you a cool $1 million. Deal?

Penniless Athletes

The Top Five Most Broke Athletes

5. Dorothy Hamill – Filed for bankruptcy following a series of financial disasters because of alleged poor guidance from advisors.

4. John Unitas – Filed for bankruptcy in 1991.

3. Latrell Sprewell – Made tens of millions as an NBA player, but recently published reports state a yacht he owned was repossessed, at least one home was foreclosed upon, and he owes tens of thousands in unpaid taxes.

2. Jack Clark – Boston Red Sox player who, in 1992, filed for bankruptcy in the middle of a multi-year, multi-million dollar contract. Among the listings in his bankruptcy petition to the court: 18 cars.

1. Mike Tyson – Declared bankruptcy and had almost $30 million in debts. One reason why: He once spent almost $10,000 to care for a tiger. Yes, a real tiger.

Fiscal Geniuses

Five Athletes Who Could Manage Your 401(k)

5. **Derek Jeter** – Cut a deal with the IRS for back taxes owed on a condo. Notice he paid the debt because he had the cash. Lots of cash.

4. **Peyton Manning** – Ad pitchman who earns millions but is known to be fiscally responsible.

3. **Floyd Mayweather Jr.** – A boxer worth a lot who saves a lot.

2. **LeBron James** – Is friends with Warren Buffett. James is so wealthy and smart he might one day have more money than Buffett.

1. **Tiger Woods** – Possibly the wealthiest ever and is also a smart saver.

This is the most unfortunate part: Holyfield had 11 kids by three different women, a level of baby-momma-making that's Shawn Kemp-ian. Reports say Holyfield pays $500,000 a year annually in child-support payments. Holyfield, by all accounts, takes care of his children, but the question remains: how good can a father be when the situation is so dysfunctional?

Unfortunately, boxers have a long, sordid history of getting ripped off by managers as well as a notorious knack for a lack of fiscal self-control. Holyfield is one of the few jerks for which—gulp—we actually feel a twinge of sympathy. He didn't kill anyone or beat up a wife or shoot somebody. He's simply spent himself into oblivion.

Leonard Little

Somewhere in a St. Louis cemetery, there is a woman named Susan Gutweiler.

Most people have never heard of Susan. She's like many victims of drunk drivers. To some, she's a statistic, another senseless fatality among many killed by drunk drivers every year. Her death in October 1998 is slightly different, however, because she was killed by football player Leonard Little.

Little had spent much of the day celebrating his birthday by drinking. The mistake was that Little decided to get into his car and drive. He seated himself in his massive Lincoln Navigator—legally drunk—and started to drive. He approached an intersection that had a red light. Little ran the light and sped through the intersection at a high rate of speed. Gutweiler, of course, had a green light and no idea that a drunken fool was driving toward her in a car much larger than hers.

Little's car plowed into Gutweiler's car. She didn't stand a chance.

After the accident, Little pled guilty to involuntary manslaughter and received 90 days in prison, four years of probation, and 1,000 hours of community service. Little should've felt fortunate. It seemed like such a light sentence for killing someone.

Along with many other members of the media, I heard Little speak when his team, the St. Louis Rams, reached the Super Bowl in 2000. Reporters packed in around him, and Little seemed genuinely contrite. I remember thinking: what he did was awful, but at least it seems Little is determined not to let anything like that ever happen again. "I think about it all the time," Little said. "I mean every day I wake up in the morning I think about it. It's always in the back of my mind no matter if you're at the Super Bowl or anything bigger than that. It's always there and I always think about it."

Now, of course, we all know Little was totally full of it.

Six years later, while driving 78 mph in a 55-mph stretch of highway in Missouri, according to police, Little was stopped and police maintain he reeked of alcohol and flunked not one but three different sobriety tests. When the case went to court, it was decided that police didn't follow proper procedures in administering the tests, and many of the drunk driving charges were thrown out. Little was sentenced to two years probation and ordered to not consume alcohol. Little again escaped with a ridiculously light sentence. Being ordered not to drink? As Derrick Coleman might say: whoop-de-damn-do.

The Little case truly makes you wonder just how much of a break he received because of his athlete status. Please don't think this book is a rant against athletes. Most of them are decent human beings who follow the rules and respect the law. Little isn't one of them. While alcoholism is a definite illness, Little still had control over whether or not he got into an automobile after drinking.

The irony? Little is still playing. Incredibly, he's still playing football after killing someone.

George Brett

Now, while we are sometimes a bit persnickety and—as right-wingers might call us, a tad uppity—we are still a little hardcore at times. We keep it real, somewhere between gangsta and Barry Manilow. Yet even we have never heard a story like this. Never, ever. We never will, either. It would be impossible. It'd be like Pacman Jones trying to avoid strippers.

In 2008, a video surfaced of former baseball great George Brett speaking to a small group of Kansas City Royals players. What he says is, well, unfathomable. Seriously, who would ever say these things in public? Why, George, why?

Brett talks about poop. There, we said it. Poop. Freaking poop.

A partial transcript of the video appears below. We're not sure who shot the video. No one has put in a claim. We're assuming the shooter is a proctologist.

"I [expletive] my pants last night," Brett begins. "I did…went out and had a great meal, just a great [expletive] meal. I had to go to the bathroom so bad in the car…I'm good uh, twice a year for that."

Brett then turns to a teammate, who is stretching, and asks, "When was the last time you [expletive] your pants?" The player looks stunned. The player looks like Brett just asked, "Can I sleep with your sister?" The player responds, "Yeah, it's been a long time." That's a good answer, particularly when you're a grown-ass man.

Brett continued, "I was in Vegas a couple years ago. This is an honest-to-god true story. Staying at the Bellagio and went over to the Mirage for dinner and met some friends of mine over there...gamble a little bit, had a tee time early in the morning so I said, 'Look, I gotta get going.' I'm walkin' back to the hotel and I get three quarters of the way out of the lobby all of the sudden I go, 'Aww [expletive]!' I'm standing here like this. I got my butt pinched like this so hard, I'm [expletive], I can't move.

"All of a sudden, you know, it felt alright. I went just like this and [makes a whooshing sound] water...I had food poisoning from the crabs. Take off my leather jacket. Tied it around my waist and I'm just standing there and it's just running down my leg. I got jeans on...no socks and I just start [expletive] walking, and every time I walk, something's coming out it's water. Just straight [expletive] water. Then, to show you how sick I was, then I'm standing outside and make a call on my cell phone. I call a guy. I said, 'Larry you're not gonna believe this. I'm standing outside the lobby of the Bellagio. I can't move. I got [expletive] everywhere. I got [expletive] all over myself."

Yes, indeed, Larry most certainly could not believe what he was hearing. Also, not sure who Larry is, but he deserved a small fortune for what Brett says Larry did for him as a favor.

"And Larry's about a 48 waist," continued Brett on the video, "so he brings me over a pair of pants and some towels and he comes over and meets me, I tell him where I'm standing. He finds the closest bathroom and then I get in the escalator and he kinda pretends like he drops something so no one gets behind me. He tells me where it is and he goes in there. Goes and gets the towel all wet for me. Throws it over the [expletive] stall. I take off all my [expletive] clothes, just wipe off, leave my shoes, my pants, everything, right there. The towels just right there in the stall and I'm walking barefoot, with my shirt and with his pants that are a 48 waist through the lobby like this [mimicking holding his pants up]. [G]ot up in the morning and took the most perfect double tapered [expletive] I've ever had in my life. True story. Who's the pitcher in this game?"

You tell that story and then ask who the pitcher is? Are you kidding? How can anyone think of the pitcher after reciting in such great detail The Poop Monologues?

Who says Americans have lost their creative and ingenious sides?

Gives new meaning to that entire pine tar incident, eh? Then again, crapping themselves has long been a Royals tradition. Forget that infamous pine tar debacle, Brett. This alleged incident alone puts you in the Jerk Hall of Fame.

Just remember. Never, ever tell tales about poop in public. In fact, such stories are illegal in 28 states.

Kelvin Sampson

We try not to get too worked up about cheating college coaches. After all, big-time college sports are just one huge slice of indentured servitude. Players get ripped off, most coaches skirt NCAA rules, and the band plays on. Please don't get us started on college sports.

Kelvin Sampson, however, took rule-breaking to a truly stupid level. We will recite over and over how we all make mistakes, but the smart ones do their best to learn from those mistakes. Sampson never truly absorbed that lesson.

The problem for Sampson is he didn't just get one school in trouble. He got two universities in hot water with the NCAA.

Indiana University basketball coach Kelvin Sampson answers a question during a media availability in Indiana on Thursday, October 18, 2007. Sampson refused to answer questions concerning his latest NCAA infractions. Sampson was denied a $500,000 raise, and his team lost one scholarship for the following season after violating NCAA-imposed sanctions on phone calls. (AP Photo/Michael Conroy)

Not even Barry Switzer did that. The NCAA first investigated Sampson for illegal phone calls to recruits when Sampson was coach at Oklahoma. The NCAA stated in a lengthy report that Sampson or staff members made more than 500 illegal calls to 17 separate recruits. Five hundred calls? We don't even talk that much to our wives. Why exactly would you need to speak to potential players hundreds of times? What do you talk about? "Yo brah', this is Coach Sampson," he might say. "Did you see *CSI* last night?"

Sampson was warned by the NCAA and issued serious recruiting and telephone restrictions. Now that's where Sampson should've looked in the mirror and said, "Hello. I'm Kelvin Sampson and I'm a phone-a-holic," then vowed to never make those kinds of mistakes again. But nooooooo. Sampson gets a second chance at Indiana University and engages in serial tomphonery again. The NCAA accused him of knowingly violating his probation from the Oklahoma fiasco by making more impermissible calls to recruits. There are phone sex addicts who don't use the phone this much.

A summary of the NCAA's allegations against Sampson, as detailed and written by the Associated Press:

> 1. Sampson, assistant coach Jeff Meyer, and former assistant Rob Senderoff failed to comply with sanctions imposed on Sampson for impermissible recruiting calls he made while he was the head coach at Oklahoma. Sampson and Senderoff, who resigned his position, are alleged to have jointly participated in telephone calls at a time when Sampson was prohibited from being present or taking part when staff members made recruiting calls. Senderoff and Meyer are alleged to have made about 100 calls that exceeded the sanction limits.
>
> 2. Senderoff and Meyer placed "at least 25 telephone calls" to nine potential recruits that exceeded NCAA limits even if no sanctions had been in place.
>
> 3. Sampson "acted contrary to the NCAA principles of ethical conduct when he knowingly violated recruiting restrictions imposed by the NCAA Committee on Infractions."
>
> 4. Sampson and Meyer engaged in an impermissible recruiting contact during a two-day sports camp.

There was also some nonsense about the NCAA being upset over a recruit receiving an impermissible benefit: a T-shirt and backpack. Now that one is absolutely ridiculous. It's a freaking T-shirt.

The phone calls are ridiculous, sure, but the worst part is Sampson failing to learn from his mistake and appreciate his second chance. That failure led to Sampson getting a second school in deep trouble.

Hal McRae

Before the explosion heard in the Pegasus galaxy, Hal McRae initially looked fairly calm. When he sat down to do a postgame interview on April 26, 1993, following a loss to the Detroit Tigers, McRae at first barely raised his voice. McRae discussed how he wanted his left-handed batters to hit better. Then he was asked a question, a normal baseball question about substituting one player for another, when all heck broke loose.

There was something clearly bottled up inside McRae waiting to erupt. Then again, he was the manager for the Kansas City Royals, a team that has caused many a decent manager to lose their minds. McRae's outburst happened so quickly, and reached such a magnificent fever pitch, it caught the half-dozen or so journalists attending the new conference totally by surprise. It took place in a small room, and McRae started tossing everything that was in his path. He was Hurricane Hal. The video of the outburst remains a stunning visual. The phone McRae tossed actually hit one of the reporters in the face, causing blood to run down his right cheek. Once the objects tossed by McRae started to fly, the members of the media began scurrying like someone was offering a free buffet in another room.

Players and team officials shut the door to McRae's office, hoping that would calm him down, or lock him in, but McRae kept cursing. He sounded like Redd Foxx. Refusing to allow a simple door to stop him, he came out of the office and screamed some more. He ended the tirade by saying, "Put that in your [expletive] pipe and smoke it."

Awesome conclusion. Tirades don't get much better than that. It was one minute and 25 seconds of pure fury and amusement.

McRae's meltdown might not be the best. Dennis "They Are Who We Thought They Were" Green's or Jim Mora's are the top two. McRae's is a classic though, one of the great originals. He's sort of the Red Grange of sports tirades.

Fuzzy Zoeller

Fuzzy Zoeller is a fascinating jerk. He's seen by many as a fun-loving dork. The golfing goofball. Look, it's Fuzzy being silly. Look, it's Fuzzy making a goof. Fuzzy's making a wisecrack. Fuzzy's wearing a funny hat. Fuzzy's name is Fuzzy. What a kidder, that Fuzzy.

Yet there is something unmistakably jerky about Zoeller if not phony. Like his good friend, John Daly, Zoeller's image doesn't always match reality. First, Zoeller likes to sue people. Of course, there's nothing funnier than lawsuits. He's launched into legal mode at least twice that we are aware of and maybe more. One was against a Florida newspaper and the other was against Wikipedia. Both, in our opinion, were totally unwarranted pieces of legal garbage. Now that's our opinion. Zoeller may try to sue us under the Anti-Jerk Defamation Act. Yet as far as we can remember, there is still freedom of speech in America (the Star Spangled Banner plays in the background).

We basically think Zoeller is not the happy-go-lucky Fuzzy some people think he is. In our opinion, he's a thin-skinned, athlete-baby used to hand holding, and when the heat comes his way, he reacts by hiding behind a lawyer (just like his good friend Daly).

Most golf fans (and even players on the PGA Tour) don't know about Zoeller's lawsuits. They don't know about his attempts to strangle free speech ("O beautiful, for spacious skies...") They only see the goofy Zoeller, not the mean-spirited one. Some in the golf media act as enablers in protecting the images of golfers (which is different than many in the media who cover the NFL or NBA). The curtain on the PGA Tour is rarely pulled back, whereas in the NFL we read about the foibles of Pacman Jones every day. Golf players get a major pass. On the rare occasion that some intrepid reporter does do some serious analysis, reporting, or major opinion piece, the golfer and his lawyers (as is the case with Zoeller) launch themselves via catapult into court.

(Please don't misunderstand. This isn't lawyer bashing, this is jerk bashing. Our mom is an attorney, and we love our mom. She's the best. Since we love our mom we ostensibly love lawyers.)

We have some sympathy for Zoeller. What happened to his Wiki page was wrong. It was vandalized by a punk, and Zoeller discovered who did it and sued. But hell, my Wiki page has been atrociously vandalized by bigots, psychos, and rednecks worldwide. It got so bad at one point that Wiki locked the page. But I didn't sue anybody, and I probably could have. You discover that when you write for the public, a few too many people have been visited by the crazy fairy. There are whack jobs and weirdos out there. You don't sue them. You grow thick skin.

Zoeller is particularly hypocritical in light of what's one of the most infamous outbursts in sports history. Zoeller called Tiger Woods "that little boy" and instructed Woods not to order fried chicken or collard greens for a post-Masters Champions Dinner.

First of all, we'll say it. Black people eat collards. So what. Goddamn, they're good. Given the choice between eating a banana split and collards, I'm eating collards. Given the choice of seeing Halle Berry in a bathing suit and the collards, I'm taking the collards. Plus, collards are a super food. So there's that. But none of that means I need to hear some smarmy jerk use the gentle and helpless collard as a racially tinged weapon.

Zoeller made his comments after Woods became the first African American (though he's actually a smorgasbord of races) to win a major. Something about this fact set off Zoeller's Cablanasian alarm, and he immediately went to Stereotype DefCon One.

"That little boy is driving well and he's putting well," Zoeller said at the time. "He's doing everything it takes to win."

Beautiful.

"So you know what you guys do when he gets in here?" Zoeller continued. "You pat him on the back and say congratulations and enjoy it and tell him not to serve fried chicken next year. Got it?" No one on the Jerk Council really eats friend chicken. We're watching our cholesterol. Plus, it's too messy.

If someone dared say the equivalent about Zoeller that Zoeller said about Woods, Zoeller would've sued.

What's comical about the monologue is the end. Zoeller snaps his fingers and does this weird thing with his head and hips. It was his way, we believe, of saying, "Oh, snap!" It's like Zoeller saw someone say it on television (maybe one night while channel surfing he came across *Def Comedy Jam*) but was too unhip and uncoordinated to fully imitate it.

Zoeller issued some semblance of an apology, but the damage to his reputation and jerk status was irreversible. Meanwhile, that lawsuit he filed against a Florida newspaper we mentioned before? When a writer from the paper (a very good one in fact) wrote a parody of Zoeller's remarks, Zoeller sued. Unbelievable.

If you do something stupid—and we have—mocking abuse is inevitable. You just have to take it. You don't sue.

You don't sue like a coward.

The Coolest White People in Sports

Top 5 Coolest White People in Sports (otherwise known as the white people who would never say anything bad about blacks— in other words, the anti-Zoellers.)

5. **David Stern** – He's commissioner of the NBA, for goodness sake.

4. **Tony Kornheiser** – The only thing he hates is traveling by airplane.

3. **David Beckham** – Just seems cool as hell.

2. **Steve Nash** – Canadians love everyone.

1. **Dan Patrick** – Coolest white guy on the planet. By far. And it's not because he's had us on his radio show. Or maybe it is. Just a little.

Bobby Petrino

Pat Forde from ESPN.com may have summed up Bobby Petrino better than anyone ever has or ever will when he wrote the following in what was a scathing column on the gypsy coach. Forde was writing to Arkansas football fans. Petrino had just bolted from the Atlanta Falcons for the Razorbacks.

"The disingenuous drifter doesn't love you or any other fan base," Forde wrote. "He doesn't love any school or any NFL franchise. He loves himself, his playbook, and his bank account. That's it. Don't expect it to change."

Ouch. That's harsh.

But very true.

Petrino is football's version of Larry Brown only he actually might be much worse. He's worse than Nick Saban, no question. Yes, he puts Nick Freaking Saban's überdouchebaggery to shame.

The problem remains the hypocrisy of college coaches (and to a much smaller degree professional coaches as well) who can move at will while the NCAA puts restrictions on the players that would make Moscow proud. College coaches want commitments, request loyalty, demand it actually, from the players, and then bolt at the first moneymaking opportunity.

There's nothing wrong with earning money. This is a socialist, er, capitalist society. It's obscene, however, to severely restrict the movements of players while coaches move at will with few restrictions or penalties.

Petrino takes this to a new level. Forde details his transgressions in painstaking detail, and they are truly amazing. One of the more egregious was how in his first year as Louisville coach—first year, mind you—he attempted to negotiate a deal to become coach at Auburn two days before Louisville's final regular-season contest. Initially, Petrino lied about the meeting then admitted the truth and asked for forgiveness. The fan base gave it to him.

One year later, Petrino interviewed for the Mississippi, Notre Dame, and Florida jobs, just months after declaring his love for all things God and Louisville. Petrino, after those interviews, again said he was staying at Louisville.

"I want to make it clear that I'm not interested in any other coaching jobs and am happy at the University of Louisville," Petrino told the media. "I'm very excited about our move into the Big East, the opportunity to play in a BCS bowl game, and the chance to compete for a national championship. [School president] Dr. James Ramsey and Tom Jurich, through their hard work and dedication, have made this the best job in the country.

As I've stated before, Louisville is the perfect place to raise a family, and I plan for all four of my children to graduate from high school in Louisville."

Notice: Petrino used his own kids as sort of collateral to try and convince his fans he loved Louisville. Remember that as we proceed to just a few weeks later when he interviewed for the LSU job. Boy, those kids sure did graduate quickly!

Just a short time afterward he interviewed with the Oakland Raiders. He turned down the Raiders and in 2006 signed a huge contract with Louisville that as Forde explains contained a $1 million buyout. "We did want to make a statement," Petrino told the media, referring to the buyout clause. "I wanted to make sure everyone understood—I know I've said it—that this is where I want to be, where my family wants to be. But I want everyone to really believe it."

Soon after that, he was gone to the Atlanta Falcons.

The Falcons knew Petrino's disgraceful history and deserved what happened to them next. He quit on the Falcons after only one season and even after telling owner Arthur Blank that he wasn't interested in college jobs and was coming back to the Falcons. He blatantly lied to Blank and departed for Arkansas. Well, departed isn't exactly the right word. He slipped out under the cover of darkness, gutlessly, shamelessly.

Instead of telling the players to their faces, he left a note in their lockers. "Out of my respect for you, I am letting you know that, with a heavy heart, I resigned today as head coach of the Atlanta Falcons," Petrino wrote. "This decision was not easy, but it was made in the best interests of me and my family. While my desire would have been to finish out what has been a difficult season for us all, circumstances did not allow me to do so. I appreciate your hard work and wish you the best."

What, no mention of kids graduating from high school?

"Disloyal," said Falcons player Jamaal Anderson. "If he can leave players here, what makes you think he won't leave the players he's going to coach? I'm just afraid to see what happens if he does bad at Arkansas. Is he going to leave those kids?"

Excellent question.

"Everything he preached over the past eight months was a lie," Atlanta player Lawyer Milloy told the press at the time. "Everything he said he stood for was a lie. He came in and messed with a lot of people's lives—he wasted a year of my life. It was a cowardly act. A selfish act."

As of this moment, Petrino is still at Arkansas saying it is the place he always wanted to be and always will be, forever and ever, "Woo Pig Sooie," amen.

He's staying until his kids graduate from high school.

Tomorrow.

 # Larry Johnson

Oh goody, another woman beater. Sweet joy.

Larry Johnson, NFL running back and alleged hopeless romantic.

This from the Associated Press that viewed the police report of yet another allegation against Johnson that involved some sort of abuse against a woman: "Ashley Stewart, 24, told police she had left the nightclub in Kansas City's Country Club Plaza district but re-entered around 1:45 AM to find a friend. Johnson, who had tried to buy her a drink at the same club a week earlier, asked the friend to have Stewart come over, according to the police report. Johnson got close to Stewart while swinging his arms belligerently, then said, 'All I wanted (to) tell you is I'm going to kill your boyfriend,' the report said. Johnson kept talking to Stewart and spit the drink in her face after she backed away, the report said. Stewart told police that Johnson's bodyguards then tackled her and that bouncers from the club escorted her outside. Johnson tried to spit on her three more times while walking to his car after the club manager asked him to leave, the report said."

Absolutely lovely.

Normally allegations are just that—allegations. The problem for Johnson is that as of October 2008 (when that incident happened), he'd been accused of assaulting a woman four times in the previous five years. That kind of average gets you into the Alleged Woman Beater Hall of Fame.

You wonder what would happen to regular folks if we did what athletes did. If we were accused of beating up a woman or trashing a hotel room and didn't have millions of dollars and an army of lawyers on the payroll, would we end up in jail far faster than them? Sorry, rhetorical question.

Before his alleged spit-target practice, Johnson was already in trouble. He'd been charged earlier that year and was awaiting a court date after being accused of simple assault against a woman at a club. First, why is it "simple" assault? Is there such a thing as "multi-layered" assault? Second, if we were Johnson, we'd stay the hell out of clubs because that's where he seems to get into the most trouble. In 2005, he was accused of pushing a woman to the ground at a Kansas City bar. The charges were dropped after she failed to appear in multiple court hearings. So maybe, if Johnson stayed out of bars, he'd stay out of courts. Wait, check that; we forgot about 2003 when he was charged with misdemeanor domestic battery and felony aggravated assault after waving a gun around his girlfriend during an alleged domestic incident.

Charges were dropped when he was admitted to a court-sanctioned anti-domestic violence program.

Apparently his domestic violence classes didn't take.

And yet, after all of that, Johnson still has an NFL career.

That's probably the most incredible fact of them all about Johnson.

54 Don Imus

Full admission. I'm nappy-headed. Not a ho' but I'm nappy-headed. Happy to be nappy.

That's what Don Imus called the women basketballers of Rutgers University. He called them nappy-headed hos. What Imus said was ignorant. But that's not the sole reason he's a jerk. It's not even the biggest reason.

You see, what Imus stated was stupid, but truthfully it wasn't as offensive as people made it out to be and Imus certainly shouldn't have been fired. That will surprise some of our right-wing friends. Let us repeat: he didn't deserve to be fired. Suspended, yes. Fired, no. Freedom of speech provides for leeway even if occasionally a line is crossed.

Also, while Imus rates high in schmuck factor, he's always acted like a toad. What he said about Rutgers was standard fare for his show.

Imus is truly a jerk because of the way he handled the aftermath of his comments. He groveled to civil rights leaders like Al Sharpton. He begged for forgiveness. It was in sharp contrast to the Imus who always appeared to not give a damn what others thought of him. We would've had more respect for Imus had he been, well, Imus, and told his critics to kiss his wrinkled, white ass. Instead, he got soft, and if there is one thing that drives us crazy it's soft jerks. If you're going to be a jerk—be a jerk. Don't be a pandering jerk once you say something stupid.

That's all we have to say on the matter. We're sure you got as sick of Imus as we did, so we won't belabor this. Thank you.

Signed, the nappy-headed Jerk Council.

Don Imus appeared on Rev. Al Sharpton's radio show in New York on April 9, 2007. Imus was dismissed from his syndicated program (simulcast on MSNBC) in April for calling the Rutgers University women's basketball team "nappy-headed hos." (AP Photo/Richard Drew)

Christian Peter

For once, let's talk less about a jerk and more about a hero the jerk helped to almost create. Some 17 years ago, Katherine Redmond, a petite 5'2", 120-pound woman, was attacked and raped by the 6'2", 265-pound University of Nebraska football player Christian Peter. I've had many conversations with Redmond who—full disclosure—is a close friend. Redmond's story, however, is one many people have heard and been moved by (not just me) as she was transformed from a woman assaulted by an overpowering University of Nebraska football player into a sort of civil rights leader. That metamorphosis started with Peter, who Redmond says raped her after she'd been enrolled at Nebraska for only a week. Peter lured her to his room, she remembers, and raped her, and then, the next day, did so again after bullying his way past dorm security. The second time he attacked Redmond, she says, he did so with two teammates watching the assault.

Redmond still remembers that night all these years later. What she recalls the most, as she told *The Boston Globe*, and me on many occasions, are Peter's eyes. "I told him, 'No,' both nights, and it didn't register," she said. "His eyes were very predatory. Just blank. There was nothing there. I remember that vividly. Nothing behind those eyes. It's like these terrorists; you wonder how they can do what they do. It's just a lack of conscience."

It wasn't just that violent moment that ignited Redmond's transformation. After reading about a 22-year-old woman named Akina Wilson, who in 1997 committed suicide soon after Wilson told police she'd been attacked by New York Giants defensive back Tito Wooten, Redmond was outraged. In her mind, there was a direct link between Wooten's alleged attack and Wilson's suicide (full disclosure part two: I wrote that story detailing Wooten's crimes for the *New York Times*). Redmond started the organization National Coalition Against Violent Athletes, a nonprofit group that to this day helps victims of athlete violence. Redmond and her organization have counseled hundreds of women, many of whom were physically attacked by athletes.

What Redmond has done is quite simply one of the more impressive things we've ever seen in sports. She's maintained her organization for all these years with very little fanfare, quietly helping women, many of whom were sexually assaulted.

Peter is a repeating jerk who never took his numerous second chances seriously. Nebraska coach Tom Osborne—who later apologized to Redmond for how he personally handled the assault—allowed Peter to allegedly commit numerous crimes while at Nebraska and barely corralled him. While there, Peter was arrested at least eight times and convicted four times. Some of the arrests were for public urination, grabbing a woman by the throat, trespassing, refusing to comply with police, and threatening to kill a parking attendant. Peter was also accused in 1993 of sexually assaulting a woman in her dorm room as well as groping another woman in a crowded bar.

Christian Peter, for a significant chunk of his life, was a one-man crime wave.

If it wasn't for Redmond speaking out against Peter, it's difficult to say if Peter's notorious actions would've ever been known. If Redmond also hadn't started her group, there would have been hundreds of women without a friend after facing such a traumatic event.

Plaxico Burress

There are these devices, Mr. Burress, called telephones. You won't believe this, but they allow you to converse over great distances. It's unbelievable, really. Some of these telephones, Plaxico, are even small. They can fit in your pocket. Your telephone can be mobile. No, seriously, it can. And phones work—get this—24 hours a day, seven days a week.

Telephones are your friend, Plaxico. You can trust them. They will not harm you unless you roam extensively. They do not want to take over your mind or switch bodies with you. They are pleasant and friendly, though sometimes their contracts can be a bit unyielding.

Burress was suspended in 2008 by the Giants after he failed to show up for meetings on one particular Monday. He didn't call the team with a reason why, and when the Giants phoned Burress, they couldn't locate him. Burress' agent would later say that Burress had a family emergency, but the Giants didn't buy it. Basically, anyone with a brain wouldn't believe that excuse. It's an excuse that's been used by term-paper writers for hundreds of years.

And all of this happened before Burress shot himself in the leg with his own gun.

Many things make Burress so jerk-worthy. One of the biggest is that just a short time earlier, the Giants had just handed over millions of dollars to him in a contract extension, and he repaid them by disappearing without notice. Some of these guys, frankly, are just like little children.

Then there was an item that appeared in the *New York Post.* Here's part of it: "The Giants shouldn't feel bad. They weren't alone in having a hard time getting in touch with Plaxico Burress. He also has dodged calls from Khoury Alternative Claims Management, a San Antonio-based third-party administrator trying to catch up with the Giants receiver about some damage he did to a rental car. Burress returned a Suburban on June 2 [2008] to Epic Car and Truck Rental in Clifton, N.J., with scratches and dents in the bumper. He paid $996.95 for the rental but owed another $1,759 in damages. Burress dropped the car off after hours and never informed anyone of the damages. 'A lot of people do that,' said Randy Harris, president of Khoury Alternative Claims Management. 'Because of the damage they just split.'"

But why would a professional athlete who makes millions not be able to pay for minor damage to a rental car? It makes no sense unless you believe the telephone is not your friend.

"The Giants confirmed they had been contacted by Harris about the issue but refused comment," the story continued. "This is similar to what the Giants often deal with regarding Burress, who has frustrated the team when he has blown off his responsibilities. Epic could not get the money from Burress and sent the matter to Khoury. 'He put down Allstate as his insurance and when we contacted them they said they don't have a policy for him,' Harris said. Repeated attempts by Khoury to contact Burress were unsuccessful and representatives from Khoury finally called the Giants, getting hold of Charles Way, the team's director of player development. 'He said he'd try his best to speak to Plaxico and get it paid,' Harris said. 'When we called him back he said, 'Man, I'm trying.'"

We know Charles Way, and he's the antithesis of Burress: smart, professional, and responsible. It must frustrate him to no end babysitting grown men.

Oh, and there's the obligatory accusations of domestic violence. It was reported by *The Bergen Record* that in 2008, police were called to Burress' home twice within just a several month span following arguments between Burress and his wife. In two instances, restraining orders were sought by Burress' wife and later dismissed in state court.

We're going to guess that Burress then understood the power of the telephone. He might've needed one to call a lawyer.

The Cincinnati Bengals

It's quite possible there's never been an organization in the history of sports that was more riddled with punks, turds, and criminals than the Cincinnati Bengals. Only the Portland Jail Blazers come close, but even they are to the Bengals what Britney Spears is to Aretha Franklin.

Between April 2006 and June 2007, ten Cincinnati Bengals were arrested for a variety of crimes, according to numerous published reports. In that time span, the Bengals won eight games—meaning they had more arrests than victories. How awesome is that!

The arrestees include:

Wide receiver Chris Henry: Wide ranging misdemeanor generator including several drunk driving allegations. Henry's been arrested at least four times on various charges.

Linebacker Odell Thurman: Alleged drunk driver, suspended by the NFL for violating the league's substance abuse policy.

Defensive lineman Frostee Rucker: Alleged domestic violence.

Linebacker A.J. Nicholson: Alleged drunk driving, marijuana possession, domestic violence, among other allegedly alleged allegations incarnate.

Defensive tackle Matthias Askew: Alleged resisting arrest.

Wide receiver Reggie McNeal: Alleged resisting arrest.

Offensive lineman Eric Steinbach: Charged with boating under the influence. Navy career in jeopardy.

Running back Quincy Wilson: Arrested at a wedding reception for disorderly conduct. How do you get arrested at a wedding? You're only supposed to get arrested at the divorce.

The Bengals were so disgraceful, so disorderly, and so arrogant that they became a symbol for out-of-control athletes and a platform for NFL Commissioner Roger Goodell to launch his law and order initiative.

What we saw with the Bengals was practically unprecedented, and we'll likely never see a group like that again. Thank goodness.

50   Albert Belle

This remains one of our favorite graphs ever penned. It was written by ESPN baseball analyst Buster Olney, one of the best in the business, when Olney was writing for the *New York Times*.

In this photo provided by the Maricopa County Sheriff's Office, former major league slugger Albert Belle is shown in a booking mug shot on Thursday, February 16, 2006. Belle was sentenced to three months in jail and five years of supervised probation Thursday, Aug. 24, 2006, for stalking a woman with whom he had a "business relationship." (AP Photo/ Maricopa County Sheriff's Office)

"It was a taken in baseball circles that Albert Belle was nuts," wrote Olney. "The Indians billed him $10,000 a year for the damage he caused in clubhouses on the road and at home, and tolerated his behavior only because he was an awesome slugger. He slurped coffee constantly and seemed to be on a perpetual caffeinated frenzy. Few escaped his anger: on some days he would destroy the postgame buffet launching plates into the shower. After one poor at-bat against Boston, he retreated to the visitor's clubhouse and took a bat to teammate Kenny Lofton's boom box. Belle preferred to have the clubhouse cold, below 60 degrees, and when one chilly teammate turned up the heat, Belle walked over, turned down the thermostat, and smashed it with his bat. His nickname, thereafter, was 'Mr. Freeze.'"

Then there's this from the Associated Press in 2006: "Former major league slugger Albert Belle was sentenced to 90 days in jail and five years supervised probation...in a case where he admitted stalking. The former Major League Baseball star was sentenced by Maricopa County Superior Court Judge James

Keppel to 90 days in the county jail and five years of supervised probation after pleading guilty to stalking a Scottsdale woman. Police originally accused Belle of attaching a GPS tracking device to [the woman's] car. He was arrested…when he allegedly called the woman. Belle stopped short of calling [the woman] a former girlfriend in a statement he made in court. 'I made the mistake of having business arrangements with this woman,' he said. 'I regret that the business arrangement resulted in my spending 101 days in the Fourth Avenue Jail.' Belle's attorney, Joe Saienni, claims [the woman] was not Belle's ex-girlfriend. 'In the evidentiary hearing, it came out the [woman] was a licensed escort at one time and that was the nature of this relationship,' he said. Bell added: 'I have learned that my beautiful and wonderful wife truly loves me unconditionally as she has stuck by my side. I hope she continues to forgive me over time and our marriage will continue to grow stronger.'"

Did we read that right? He stalked a prostitute? Just a quick note, Albert. There's more than one prostitute in the world. You can select from many choices. So we hear.

Remember, Belle is the same jackass who chased trick-or-treaters off of his property. Belle isn't a jerk because he treats the media poorly. Frankly, some of us in the media deserve to be treated like horse poop. Some of us are miserable, bitter old goats. No, Belle is a jerk because of the way he treated his sport overall, as well as fans and teammates in particular. It's one thing to treat a bunch of writers like dirt. It's another to treat people in and around the sport like doormats, and Belle was Reggie Jackson–like in doing that. *New York Daily News* writer Bill Madden likely encapsulated many people's feelings about Belle when he wrote, "Sorry, there'll be no words of sympathy here for Albert Belle. He was a surly jerk before he [retired] and now he's a hurt surly jerk.… He was no credit to the game. Belle's boorish behavior should be remembered by every member of the

Baseball Writers' Association when it comes time to consider him for the Hall of Fame."

Belle deserves to be in the Hall of Fame. He should also be remembered as a foul-tempered goon. Both things will probably occur.

Art Modell

Wed don't hate Art Modell. Actually, we like him. We don't completely blame him for moving one of the most storied franchises in sports, the Cleveland Browns, to Baltimore. The blame is shared between Modell and the city of Cleveland that at one point seemed to favor keeping the Indians, Cavaliers, and the Rock and Roll Hall of Fame over the Browns.

No, we don't hate Modell. We can't since we grew up as Baltimore Colts fans and watched a greedy jerk move the Colts to Indianapolis under the darkness of night. Poof, they were gone, just like that. Then Modell gave Baltimore a team again. We can't hate him. He gave us Marylanders professional football (again) even if it wasn't the ideal way for us to get it.

We know that a lot of people do hate Modell. There are Browns fans, all these years after Modell moved the team, who wake up in the morning, step into the bathroom, and at the bottom of their toilet is a picture of Modell. If you want to grasp just how much Browns fans hate Modell, think Middle East. Think Michael Moore and George Bush.

We don't feel that hate and while, again, the true responsibility for the Browns leaving Cleveland lies with many parties, we have to assign the blame mostly to Modell because the Browns were ultimately his team. They were his team, and he made that dreaded decision.

The biggest problem we have with Modell was his continual promise to never move the Browns. He'd repeatedly criticized other NFL owners who moved their teams and vowed to never do that to the city of Cleveland. While Modell would still be hated by many Browns fans regardless, the promise to never move ignited the intense hatred in the end. Browns fans felt—and feel—that Modell lied to them. They're not wrong to feel that way.

The entire situation ultimately worked out. Cleveland has their Browns, and Baltimore has a team, as well. In some ways, what happened to Modell is sad. His legacy is utterly destroyed by an act of self-mutilation. There's a sportswriter in Cleveland who is making it his sole mission in life to keep Modell out of the Hall of Fame. Such vendettas are petty and asinine. The Hall of Fame without Modell is like eating chocolate chip cookies without beer, er, milk.

Wrote *USA Today's* Jon Saraceno: "Modell was one of 15 finalists [for the Hall of Fame]. But he failed to make the top 10 after an impassioned speech by a *[Cleveland] Plain Dealer* sportswriter who cited the Browns' controversial relocation in 1996. It has been suggested by some voters that the reporter has a vendetta against Modell." Saraceno added, "The NFL, as we know it today, could not be the league that it is without him. He was an integral, driving force behind the league's decision to equally divvy up television revenue among franchises. Along with Pete Rozelle, he helped lay the foundation that became the bedrock of league fortunes and for years was a driving force in TV negotiations. His old Browns won an NFL title and his new Ravens a Super Bowl. And he hired Ozzie Newsome, one of the first significant minority executives in team front offices. Voters shouldn't approve Modell because he is old and in poor health or because he unfailingly helped media types [and their predecessors] do their jobs or because he's good with a quip or because he's really an old softie. They should admit Art Modell because he has earned it. To freeze him from the Hall says more about the electorate than it does the man."

Modell is a jerk for moving the team, but he's one of the few jerks who deserves to be forgiven.

 # Isiah Thomas

We're not going to be our overly obnoxious and smirk-faced selves on this one because it requires the utmost of sensitivity. Wait. Hold on. We forgot. We're not sensitive. This from the *New York Daily News* in October 2008: "Disgraced ex-Knicks coach Isiah Thomas was rushed to a hospital…after overdosing on sleeping pills at his swank Westchester County mansion, sources said."

Notice the disdain dripping from that lead: "…swank Westchester County mansion, sources said."

What does a swank Westchester County mansion have to do with Thomas and alleged sleeping pills? We're not complaining, we're just wondering. The answer is nothing. It was just a way to make Thomas look stupider than he already did.

Anyone who believed that Thomas couldn't sink any lower than his miserable days as a Knicks executive and sexual harasser were sadly mistaken.

Thomas denied overdosing and who knows exactly what occurred, but it's interesting that Thomas told members of the

New York press that it wasn't him, but his daughter who took the pills. Harrison Police Chief David Hall was quoted as saying of Thomas, "Maybe the guy took a couple of pills, couldn't go to sleep, took a couple more, couldn't go to sleep—who knows? He couldn't fall asleep and took two sleeping pills. He then took two more until he took too many."

Hall added, "I understand that this person claims it was his daughter; he is lying. It was definitely not his daughter, it was a male. We know the difference between a 47-year-old black male and a young black female."

Thank God for that.

"It wasn't his daughter," Hall told the Associated Press. "And why they're throwing her under the bus is beyond my ability to understand."

Ours as well. It was another bizarre incident in the life of a small man who was arguably the greatest undersized point guard who ever lived.

When Thomas took over the Knicks as team president in 2003, it started a simultaneous erosion of the team and his reputation. His Knicks teams never won more than 33 games. He drafted horribly, picked bad free agents, and ruined the team's salary cap situation. Other than that, he was very talented.

What makes Thomas truly jerk-worthy goes beyond his putrid on-court performance. In 2006, he was sued along with Madison Square Garden for the sexual harassment of Anucha Browne Sanders. In 2007, a jury sided with Sanders and ordered the Garden to pay her $11.6 million.

That kind of cash would certainly buy a lot of Lunesta.

Thomas has been named one of the 50 greatest players in NBA history. To us, he was the greatest of the smaller points. None of them could match his intensity or defensive prowess. He was a perfect combination of nastiness and talent. He could also be a supreme dick. Despite his denials, it's our belief that he was the leader of a group of people who froze out Michael Jordan in the 1985 All-Star game, a fact Jordan never refuted (or forgave). It was a petty move all due to Thomas' jealousy over the attention a young Jordan was receiving.

There were people who read about the alleged sleeping-pill situation and felt great sympathy. There are others who—perhaps harshly or maybe not—thought karma had finally caught up to Thomas.

Bill Parcells

"I've coached my last football game. You can write that on your little chalkboard. This is it. It's over."

—BILL PARCELLS AFTER HE QUIT
THE NEW YORK JETS IN 1999

Of course, it wasn't over. First he "retired" from the New York Giants. Then he accepted a job with the Tampa Bay Buccaneers before jilting them and de-accepting. We're not even sure "de-accepting" is a word, but it fits Parcells. Then he "retired" from the New England Patriots. Then he "retired" from the Jets. Then he "retired" from the Dallas Cowboys. Each time after retiring, and sometimes before, he put himself in the mix for another job, and then he'd scream at the media for questioning his commitment to his current gig. It's ironic how one of the greatest bullies in recent sports history always seems to be running from something.

Parcells is the kind of coach who asks his players for their complete and unwavering dedication, and a short time after delivering that sort of speech, he asks his agent to see what other teams are hiring.

What Parcells did in Super Bowl XXXI was perhaps his most atrocious piece of disingenuousness of all. The Super Bowl should be a time when teams focus on, well, the Super Bowl. Imagine that: a team concentrating on its championship game. But as he often does while holding one job, Parcells was looking for an exit. The possibility of Parcells leaving the Patriots for the New York Jets was the biggest topic of conversation all that week. I know. I was there. Patriots officials privately fumed because everyone knew that Parcells was leaving, and Parcells was deceiving the public by stating he wasn't.

After the game, Parcells didn't fly home with the Patriots on the team flight; think about that. The head coach's team just lost the Super Bowl and he didn't return with them from the game. Imagine the reaction of the media if Terrell Owens ever did that. He'd be crucified.

During the week, Parcells gave the now infamous quote, "If they want you to cook the dinner, at least they ought to let you shop for some of the groceries." The line was in reference to a personnel dispute between he and owner Robert Kraft.

Amazingly, despite possessing one of the harshest attitudes toward the press in recent years by any coach (and also one of the most restrictive and punitive), many in the media constantly sought Parcells' approval. Covering Parcells was like covering a communist regime. He was one of the first coaches in the modern age that did everything in his power to limit access and information. Parcells was also one of the first to be blatantly misleading about injuries. It was Parcells, as much as any coach, who led the NFL to enact harsher standards regarding its injury reporting policies.

Often Parcells' tactic was to select one or two writers he'd confide in, then treat the others like microwaved garbage. That way, Parcells had at least one ally in the media. It would take someone with serious psychological prowess and Betazoid-like ability to deeply probe the human mind and figure out how Parcells, despite treating many in the press so horribly, was able to escape the wrath of a media that normally refuses to tolerate such abuse. The late George Young, who was the general manager of the Giants when Parcells was coaching the team, once asked me, "Why do so many reporters like Parcells when he treats them like shit?" I honestly couldn't answer him.

Mostly, Parcells the Vagabond was a hypocrite. He demanded loyalty from owners, assistant coaches, and players while almost never demonstrating the trait himself. He's the Petrino of the NFL except much, much worse—if that's possible.

 # John McEnroe

John McEnroe is one of our favorite tennis players of all time, yet he's also the tennis player we've despised the most. How can both be true? Well, it's McEnroe, after all. He easily inspires both emotions. Perfect example: ESPN quoted McEnroe explaining a decision not to attend the traditional Wimbledon winners dinner in 1981 by saying, "I wanted to spend [the night] with my family and friends and the people who had supported me, not a bunch of stiffs who were 70-80 years old, telling you that you're acting like a jerk."

John McEnroe of the United States argues a line call with the umpire during his Men's Singles semi-final match on Wimbledon's Centre Court on Friday, July 4, 1980, in London, against fellow American Jimmy Connors. McEnroe claimed that he aced Connors, but the umpire—whose decision was upheld—disagreed. (AP Photo)

McEnroe was called many things in his career: champion, all-time great, foul-mouth, and stone-cold jerk. There are few athletes who embody that last word better than McEnroe. He was called by a British tabloid, "the most vain, ill-tempered, petulant loudmouth that the game of tennis has ever known." Wrote the *Washington Post*: "He came across as a precocious brat—immensely talented, spoiled, and rather obnoxious. On the court, he pouted, cursed, threw his racket....He was a crybaby. Off court, he demonstrated little *savoir faire*." We're not even sure what *savoir faire* means—it's either a song by Chic or a sexually transmitted disease—but you know a guy is a jerk when the jerk's own father says he's a jerk.

"John sets high standards for himself and doesn't suffer fools gladly," John Sr. told ESPN. "What you might say about John is that he shoots from the hip through his mouth."

The irony is that if McEnroe had done less screaming at tennis officials and behaved more like a decent human being instead of a boorish jackass, he could've been one of the most popular athletes in U.S. sports history and an endorsement king. Only now is McEnroe cashing in with advertisers all these years after his controversial career ended.

45   Ray Lewis

Everything changed for Ray Lewis in January 2000. Lewis was attending a Super Bowl party in Atlanta when two people were stabbed and murdered. Lewis was questioned by police and asked if he knew the two main suspects in the stabbing, and he made a terrible mistake. He lied and said no. At that point, the clock was ticking; police knew Lewis was lying. Lewis was later indicted for aggravated assault and murder.

Anyone who possesses a fully functioning frontal lobe knows you don't lie to the police in a murder investigation. You don't talk about Fight Club, and you don't lie to the police when they are trying to find killers.

One of the lasting images of Lewis was his being arraigned wearing prison garb instead of his Baltimore Ravens uniform. It was a shocking sight.

Lewis likely didn't deserve to be indicted for murder. The move by prosecutors was probably a tactic to force Lewis to tell them what he actually knew. It worked. Lewis changed his story and said he indeed knew the two men. Eventually, the murder charges were dropped, and Lewis pled guilty to obstruction of justice. The NFL and Commissioner Paul Tagliabue fined Lewis $250,000 for lying to the police. At the time, it was a record-setting punishment.

Lying to police in a murder investigation is a sin that should rank Lewis higher in jerk annals. Yet part of his story is also somewhat inspirational. It was thought Lewis would never repair his reputation, but in many ways, he's since recovered (you have to remember how bad it was for him). Lewis is far from perfect, and many NFL fans will never forgive him (and we're not saying they should), but Lewis is an example of how some players know what it takes to return from the abyss while others never learn. It's a lesson Michael Vick will have to absorb very soon.

 Spain

In the United States, we have our own problems with race. Yes, that's breaking news. We know you're stunned. We have our problems, but we're nothing like some countries and sports fans in Europe, particularly Spain. Spain is to racists what Jim Crow is to rednecks. You know a country has problems when it ranks ahead of China on the jerk list.

Spain demonstrated unique racial insensitivity several times in a short span in 2008. The first moment came during the summer Olympics. The Spanish basketball team posed for a photo making a slant-eyed gesture with the fingers on their eyes. It was an openly racist gesture in reference to their upcoming opponents, the Chinese basketball team.

Imagine the reaction in this country and around the world if the Americans had made that gesture. It'd be a mess. The French would be attempting to invade us right now, and conservatives in the United States would be declaring racial double standards. In Spain, the media didn't make an issue of the gesture until other journalists from around the world did, and when the Spanish media did discuss the photo, they downplayed it. Incredibly, the Spanish women's Olympic basketball team did the exact same pose for a photo.

One website, rumorsandrants.com, has obsessively chronicled Spain's bigotry and racism when it comes to sports. It's quite a list beginning with something we've never heard of before. Wrote the site in the summer of 2008: "For its next two home Champions League games, Spanish giants Atletico Madrid will not be able to play at its own stadium. UEFA, the sport's European governing body, levied its heaviest punishment to date in banning Atletico Madrid from playing at the Vicente Calderon Stadium because of the club's fans' racist actions during last month's match between Atletico and Marseille, of France's Ligue 1. Monkey chants were aimed at Marseille's black players, insults were directed toward black journalists inside the press box, and the team bus was attacked by Madrid supporters following the match. Atletico Madrid's coach Javier Aguirre also received a two-game ban for repeatedly swearing at Marseille midfielder Mathieu Valbuena, calling him a 'son of a whore.' The Spanish club was fined 150,000 euros and will have to play games against Liverpool...and PSV Eindhoven...at least 300 kilometers outside of Madrid. UEFA added that if there is another racist outburst in the next five years, more matches will be moved."

Soccer fans in Europe are so passionate about their sport they make SEC football fans look like kindergartners. In Spain, it seems, they love soccer but hate soccer players who happen to be black.

Before the 2004 World Cup game against France, Luis Aragones, the Spanish coach, called French striker Thierry Henry a "black shit." Aragones didn't say Henry *took* a black shit. He said he *was* a black shit. Big difference. In mid-2008, a rising star in Formula One, who is black, was taunted by a group of Spanish fans that had painted black faces and bodies and screamed racist slurs at the driver. The photo of the group made its way around the entire world.

Again, America is far from innocent, but it seems the Spanish still revel in bigotry while we're at least fighting to crawl out of that primordial muck.

Diego Maradona

We remember seeing Diego Maradona on television some years ago. He was frumpy, literally around 300 pounds, and was built like a *South Park* character. He'd been battling cocaine and alcohol addictions. We remember saying, "God, he looks like ass." It wasn't just the hardcore drugs. Maradona was physically huge. It was as if he'd declared a jihad on chocolate donuts. Many Maradona followers (including us) were startled.

We shouldn't have been. Maradona has long been a perplexing individual. Few athletes in sports history, in any history, displayed such physical grace. His most incredible goal, called by many "The Goal of the Century," happened against England in the 1986 World Cup. In another life, Maradona was a wide receiver.

Accompanying that grace was a lack of respect, at times for himself, his sport, and many people in it. Maradona was a rock star and acted like it. In 1991, he was suspended for more than a year after failing a drug test for cocaine. He failed another drug test for the metabolism kick-starter ephedrine. He was a womanizer who treated an adoring press with great disdain.

The irony is that in October 2008, Maradona was appointed head coach of the Argentina national soccer team. Now he may have to coach a greatly talented knucklehead, just like he was.

Bill Romanowski

About five years ago, I approached Bill Romanowski when he was playing for the Denver Broncos. He was sitting at his locker and was briefly alone. We talked for about five minutes, and the man couldn't have been more gentlemanly. He was thoughtful and almost eloquent in his explanation to me about some of the defenses the Broncos were playing. I remember thinking: maybe the image of this guy is wrong, maybe he's not the jerk some thought he was. Among the many idiotic things I've thought and done, that might be the dumbest.

Romanowski is a thug. There's no other way to put it. In the annals of dirty, unscrupulous football players, he'll go down as one of the dirtiest, most unscrupulous, and morally bankrupt jerks of them all. Romanowski made Conrad Dobler look like John Paul II.

"I felt I could take myself to a place where other guys weren't willing to go because come Sunday after a game, I already started hating the next opponent. I started hating the guy I was going to go against," Romanowski once told CBS News. "I hated the coaches. I hated their fans. I hated their family. You name it. And by the time I got onto that field come Sunday, watch out because there was rage."

In one respect, unlike other jerks, Romanowski always knew what he was. In that way, he was a forthright jerk, at least. That's about the only nice thing you can say about Romo, however. The number of cheap shots and disgusting tactics issued by

Romanowski is legendary. He's in many ways the 21st century version of Dobler.

Football is a terribly violent sport, but even in football a line can be crossed and Romo didn't just cross it, he truly enjoyed crossing it. There was often no remorse for his actions—or if remorse was expressed, it didn't seem all that sincere.

Romanowski wrote an autobiography *Romo: My Life on the Edge* and wrote of a scene where he was playing the Giants and

---

Playin' Dirty
The 10 Dirtiest Players in History

10. Rodney Harrison – In a 2006 survey of 361 players by SI.com, 23 percent voted Harrison the dirtiest player in the sport.

9. Jack Tatum – Paralyzed Daryl Stingley.

8. Roger Clemens – Headhunter ranked in the top 10 for hit batters.

7. Don Drysdale – Was Roger Clemens before Roger Clemens.

6. Dennis Rodman – Head-butter.

5. Mike Tyson – Ear-biter.

4. Ty Cobb – Used his spiked cleats as weapons.

3. Marty McSorley – Suspended one year by the NHL and convicted of assault for a hit to the head of Donald Brashear.

2. Conrad Dobler – Spit, kicked, gouged, and hit defenseless players in the solar plexus. One of the great cheap-shot guys of all time.

1. Bill Romanowski – Surprise choice for worst of all time but well earned.

Just missing the top 10 – Dale Earnhardt Sr., Bruce Bowen, Andre Waters, Bill Laimbeer, and John Stockton.

---

after a tackle was in the middle of a pile with running back Dave Meggett. "I am pissed," he said. "And I am down there just trying to rip that ball out of his hands. And all I could get was a finger. And at the time I thought it was his. But, just, whatever it was...I just snapped it. And I could hear a scream at the bottom of the pile." He broke the jaw of Carolina Panthers quarterback Kerry Collins and received a $20,000 fine. He spat in the face of wide receiver J.J. Stokes, and in 2003 engaged in a brutal training-camp fight with his own teammate, Marcus Williams, and broke Williams' eye socket. After Williams sued, Romo was forced to pay $415,000 in a financial settlement.

Romo has always denied steroid rage was the source of these extremely angry incidents, but it sure does sound like typical 'roid rage to us. He has admitted to using other performance-enhancers.

Romanowski is now a football coach at a high school, and that's quite frightening. Romo's actually teaching kids.

We Interrupt These Jerks

Let's take a break from jerk chronicling for something completely different: a solution.

You may have noticed that many of our jerks have problems with their temper and women. There's nothing worse than a woman beater. Yet a good number of our lovely jerks seemed to have missed that memo.

Some time ago, I authored a six-point plan to curb athlete violence against women. It's worth mentioning here again in its totality. That plan would still work today as leagues have done very little to curb this kind of pathetic nonsense. The plan is as follows:

1. An initial conviction for violence against a woman, domestic or otherwise, or a plea bargain involving such a crime, would result in a year-long suspension without pay. During the suspension, the player would receive extensive counseling, the league would monitor his compliance with protective orders, and the player would also pay for victim counseling.

   Seems excessive? Consider that a first-time steroid abuser in the NFL is suspended for four games. So does it make sense that an NFL player, for example, can be suspended for using an illegal herbal supplement but not for striking a woman?

2. A player who feels he's been wrongly accused or convicted in court can appeal to an independent arbitrator agreed upon by the unions and sports leagues. The arbitrator would investigate, with expenses being paid by taking 1 percent of a league's television revenue and placing the money in an interest-bearing account, which would provide an arbitrator with a budget of millions of dollars per year, thus funding his or her expenses and investigative staff. The arbitrator would decide the player's administrative appeal, or in essence, his fate. Lastly, the arbitrator would have domestic violence training.

   If the arbitrator upholds the court verdict, the player would be suspended. But if he or she uncovers evidence that convinces him the player shouldn't have been convicted, then the particular league would have to pay the player treble damages for pain and suffering. The league would also take out ads on websites, television, and in newspapers saying the player was exonerated.

   Lie-detector tests would also be used to prevent the unthinkable: a couple faking an attack to collect money from the NFL. Such examinations are not infallible, but

THE ALL-TIME BIGGEST SPORTS JERKS

when combined with the skills of a competent investigator, lie-detection testing can be an invaluable tool. Such tests are routinely utilized by our country's intelligence services, such as the National Security Agency.

This second step is needed because, even in domestic violence cases, the court system can make mistakes— witnesses lie and evidence is tainted or fabricated.

3. A second conviction or guilty plea for domestic violence would result in a lifetime ban from the sport. The same appeals process would apply.

4. If a team signs a player with a previous conviction or suspension for domestic abuse and the player is convicted a second time, the team would face a $5 million fine and $5 million salary cap penalty. Hitting professional teams in their pocketbook should require them to become more accountable, and hitting them in the salary-cap kneecap would require them to totally rethink signing a woman beater. Too many teams still gamble on woman beaters. These players tend not to be weeded out but circulate throughout the leagues like stale air in a condo.

The gap in this portion of the plan is apparent when dealing not with team sports but individual sports. How would you punish, say, the PGA Tour for tolerating a woman-beating golfer? To be honest, I don't have the answer. I was taught it's okay to say, "I don't know." And hell, I don't know.

5. Develop a hotline for victims of domestic violence. An independent office or non-profit organization would run it. Accusations would be quietly and professionally investigated. The player's team wouldn't be notified unless the investigators discovered proof of abuse. People

specifically trained in the field of intimate partner violence would operate the hotline and would also offer resources to victims, including shelter, support, referrals, and advocacy.

6. Sports leagues should track the names of players who've had restraining orders against them. Already, most leagues try to keep the identities on file, but the effort isn't truly organized or efficient. Police and sports leagues often don't cooperate.

These suggestions are far from perfect and there are holes in them, mostly due process, double jeopardy, and equal protection under the law issues. But something more needs to be done. The leagues are failing to slow down the athlete woman-beating nation.

Now back to our regularly scheduled jerks.

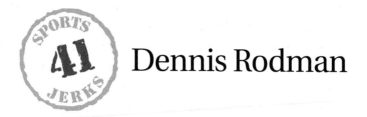

41 Dennis Rodman

Dennis Rodman wore a dress.

This jerk synopsis is going to be extremely brief because when a man wears a wedding dress, well, that's all you need to know about his jerk-worthiness. A grown man wore a wedding dress. There are many other jerk qualities that make Rodman prime jerk material (including a no-contest plea to misdemeanor spousal abuse charges), but do we really need to discuss other reasons?

He wore a dress.

Thank you. Good night.

Chicago Bulls basketball forward Dennis Rodman, dressed as a bride, poses for photographers at a Manhattan bookstore on Wednesday, August 21, 1996. Rodman was promoting his book, Bad As I Wanna Be. *(AP Photo/ Mark Lennihan)*

Lawrence Taylor

What do a pair of handcuffs, cocaine addiction, unmitigated violence, womanizing to a level that would make Jude Law blush, and almost unparalleled physical ability equal?

It equals Lawrence Taylor—the greatest defensive player of all time and Pro Bowl jerk.

Throughout most of his unbelievable and impossible playing career, Taylor possessed balls of uranium and morals with the composition of angel hair pasta.

Taylor loses jerk points for recently cleaning up his life; the drugs and addictions seem to be gone. Emphasis on *seem to be.* Still, his life was such a devastating train wreck for so long he accumulated more than enough leeway to establish jerk supremacy. No one lived life harder in the history of sports than Taylor. No one. No one exemplified excess and greatness the way Taylor did. Taylor makes Mike Tyson look like Laura Bush.

The truth about Taylor is that for all of that greatness, there was also vastly wasted talent. Taylor cheated himself and his team. The examples are numerous. He once showed up to a game with handcuffs attached to his wrists (Taylor says he appeared in a practice with the handcuffs; several Giants players say it was a game). What is not in dispute is that Taylor spent the night with two women. Taylor tells the story differently, but his former teammates say it goes this way. The women drugged Taylor and robbed him of all of his belongings except a fur coat and handcuffed him to the bed. When he awoke, he was naked and cuffed. A Giants official was able to free Taylor from the bed, but no one had the key to the handcuffs. So the handcuffs were taped over, these teammates say, and Taylor played in the game. Thus, Taylor gave new meaning to the phrase "handcuffing a defense."

Taylor was known to drink heavily before practices and games. He tested positive for cocaine twice in two years. The drug became as much a part of his life as the quarterback sack. Taylor went through drug rehabilitation twice after multiple arrests for purchasing cocaine from undercover cops. He once described his own home as a crack house. And in typical jerk fashion, Taylor was even arrested for failing to pay child support that led to him spending 12 hours in jail. Taylor was so broke at one point that the late New York Giants owner, Wellington Mara, quietly paid for one of Taylor's rehab sessions.

Some jerk stories have a happy ending. Taylor is no longer a drug-addicted punk who doesn't pay his child support. His life is much more calm and filled with golf instead of coke. And there are no handcuffs anywhere in sight.

 # Bobby Fischer

A January 18, 2008, *New York Times* obituary on chess fiend Bobby Fischer described him meticulously and accurately: "Fischer's taking of the World Championship from Boris Spassky in 1972 was hailed as a symbolic moment for American hopes in the Cold War, and in many ways, Fischer's story epitomized the self-reliant, frontier ideals of America," wrote the newspaper. *(It also inspired Chess, the musical.)* "Yet Fischer was a deeply disturbed man, and the dream evaporated after his victory in Reykjavik. Dramatically, Fischer renounced chess after failing to agree terms for his defense of the title and did not play a single competitive game for 20 years. Instead he descended into paranoia, characterized by hate-filled and poisonously anti-Semitic outbursts against his own country."

There has never been an athlete initially hailed as an American hero and then, almost as quickly, denounced as a scurrilous, loony anti-Semite.

Fischer was among the angriest jerks of them all. That is, if you discount the murdering jerks. Of the non-murdering jerks, Fischer was the angriest. It's easy to blame his anger and bouts of anti-Semitism on chemical imbalances in what was obviously a brain that functioned at an extremely high level but also had frightening, dark crevices. The problem is that Fischer started seeing conspiracies very early on in his chess career. He accused opponents of ganging up on him and withdrew from the chess world in repetitive and paranoid huffs.

He pouted and strutted and needed to be persuaded to play in big matches. In his World Championship match with Spassky, he had to be convinced to play by Henry Kissinger. Imagine if Randy Moss got a call from Condoleezza Rice pleading with him to play the New York Giants.

Fischer's descent into nuttiness was quick and steep. After mostly abandoning chess, he occasionally emerged with some sort of racist or anti-American statement. Fischer's racism wasn't subcutaneous, either. He condemned the "stinking Jews" and accused them of wanting to control the world. He disgustingly said the Holocaust was a "money-making invention." Consider that statement for a moment.

After the attacks of September 11, he went on Filipino radio and declared them a great success. His only problem with the attacks? In Fischer's mind, Al-Qaeda didn't go far enough. "Wonderful news," he said of the attacks. "It is time to finish off the U.S. once and for all."

Fischer lived the final years of his alternately brilliant and miserable life in Iceland, where he died of kidney failure. Some would say it was his heart that ultimately failed.

Scott Boras

In a small number of instances, admittedly, jerkdom resembles truthiness in that jerkiness is in the eye of the beholder. One man's jerk is another man's hero. Or is it one man's hero is another man's jerk? We digress. In some rare cases, jerkiness is corporeal. In some cases, it's debatable. In some cases, it does not lead to invective and fistfights.

Scott Boras is not one of those cases.

If you look up "jerk" in the dictionary, you'll find a picture of Boras, smiling, standing triumphantly, a wad of cash in one hand, the sport of baseball's testicles in the other.

In a one-billion-trillion-word story on Boras in *The New Yorker* titled "The Extortionist," author Ben McGrath captured the essence of Boras with these three fat paragraphs:

"Last December, at *Baseball America*'s annual banquet, Boras was named the game's most influential non-player in the twenty-five years since the magazine began publishing, beating out the current Major League Baseball commissioner, Bud Selig, who had recently declared the sport to be in its 'golden age,' as well as Don Fehr, the longtime head of the Players Association," wrote McGrath. "*(The most influential player was Barry Bonds, who is a former Boras client, and similarly regarded.)* I could kind of feel in the room that it was, like, 'What is this? Why is this guy up here? We're baseball people,' Boras recalls. The banquet is traditionally a feel-good event for management types, with a charitable focus and an emphasis on youth coaching and mentorship. Boras took the stage and delivered a sermon on economics. 'What I told them all was: You know what this business is about, guys? We've gone from, when I came into it, an industry that made, economically, about five hundred million dollars, and we went to a billion in 1990. We went to three billion in 2000. And now we're near six billion in 2007. What it says for all of us in this room is this: We're doing a good job with the game. We're growing the game, as it should be grown. There's a balance that's needed in the growing of the game, and I provide the balance on one side, and you provide it on the other.'

"The applause was tepid. 'You just wanted to crawl behind the curtain,' a *Baseball America* contributor told me," the story continued. "One National League manager considered walking out in protest. And yet influence, however coolly embraced, can be infectious. Boras, who is fifty-four, seems to have become impatient with mere balance-provision. This spring, he mailed a letter to Commissioner Selig, in which he outlined a proposal to alter the format of the game's most sacred ritual, the World Series. Why not make it nine games, instead of seven, he argued, and hold those extra two games—the first two games—at a neutral site? Cities all over the nation, or even the world, could compete for the honor of playing host, as with the Olympics. 'It's a fact that our game needs a forum that's akin to the Super Bowl,' Boras explained to me not long after he'd sent the letter. 'People don't go to the Super Bowl for the game. Most Super Bowl games are not competitive or good games. They go there for the event. They go there for the three-day weekend.' He described a vision of 'corporate hospitality,' including a 'gala, like the Oscars,' during which the MVP and Cy Young awards, among others, would be announced, with all the finalists present and on view, and presumably walking the red carpet in sponsored menswear. Who could argue against such a change? It would mean more money for the owners, more 'marketable content' for the media to broadcast, more attention for the stars—more everything."

The story continued with these two juicy and accurate quotes: "'He takes himself very seriously,' Fay Vincent, the former commissioner, said recently of Boras. 'I'm not surprised that he's beginning to make grandiose suggestions.' Vincent added that he thought this particular World Series suggestion was 'preposterous,' and, giving voice to a common complaint of fans and players alike, he said, 'I mean, the season goes on endlessly as it is.'"

Marvin Miller, the pioneering Players Association chief, was more acerbic. "That's a typical example of an agent forgetting what his real role is," Miller said. "He has no function whatsoever in suggesting a change in scheduling. He has absolutely nothing to say about it—not now or ever. But it's quite typical. It's a joke."

There are few greater examples of jerkdom in the annals of jerkiness than what Boras did during Game 4 of the 2007 World Series. Alex Rodriguez is Boras' überclient and slugger for the New York Yankees. Rodriguez had an option in his contract that allowed for him to leave the Yankees unfettered.

After Rodriguez insisted he would remain a Yankee, it was Boras, many people in baseball believe, who convinced Rodriguez to opt out of the last years of the deal because there was more money in free agency.

A greedy athlete and agent are about as unusual as a blonde cheerleader. Yet it's what Boras did next that put him in esteemed company in the annals of jerkdom.

Instead of announcing at a proper time that Rodriguez was opting out of his Yankees deal, Boras did the opposite. When is the proper time? Not exactly sure, but it certainly is *not during the World Series!* Not only was the announcement made during the 2007 World Series, it occurred during a clinching game. It was typical Boras, and to some degree typical Rodriguez—who has earned jerk honors himself—in that Boras is so self-centered and egomaniacal that he attempted to upstage baseball's showcase game.

The most interesting aspect of Boras' unbelievably childish act was that he informed members of the media several hours before he informed the Yankees about the intentions of Rodriguez. Let's repeat that. Boras told the Associated Press and SI.com that Rodriguez was opting out before he informed the general manager of the Yankees, Brian Cashman.

Boras thinks he is the smartest person in the room. He uses words like "precocious succubus" to impress. Boras believes he is regal, yet everyone knows that Boras and his motives are quite pedestrian. It's simple: Boras desires to be the center of baseball's universe, and he would even interrupt one of the biggest moments in all of sports if needed in order to accomplish that goal.

Boras remains successful despite generating a great deal of hate from teams in baseball because his client base is so extensive. Thus Boras is like Thanksgiving turkey. Everyone feels like they have to eat some, but after they do, they pass out in disgust.

Boras' ego has gotten so big, Dora can't explore it.

Commissioner Bud Selig was infuriated by Boras' antics during the World Series, according to several baseball officials. "Bud has cursed his name many times," said one general manager. (Maybe Selig also called Boras a jerk.) The reaction of the media was equally predictable. The sport went nuclear. It was as if Boras had suddenly been listed on a sex offender website. The raw criticism reached such a high pitch that Boras was forced to apologize. It was too late, however. Boras had sealed his fate as the worst agent in baseball history and earned a position among the upper tier of sports jerks.

In what was a great example of comeuppance, there was a rare and fleeting moment where Boras got his. After Rodriguez and Boras hit the free agent market and discovered the offers were not as rich as Boras had predicted, the two came crawling back to the Yankees. And the Yankees insisted that Boras not be included during the negotiations. He wasn't. The Yankees publicly smacking down Boras was one of the great moments in recent sports history.

Makes you almost want to be a Yankees fan—almost.

Randall Simon

His name is Randall Carlito Simon, and he is a sausage beater.

Please get your mind out of the gutter. Simon has a place in jerk and mascot history because of an incident that happened in July 2003. The Milwaukee Brewers hold a sausage race. We're not certain why they do this—they just do. It's a race in which four eager contestants wear these gigantic sausage costumes and sprint along the infield of the stadium at extreme slow motion because the sausage outfits weigh 20,000 pounds and are 8' tall. Sausage racing. So it's not Daytona. So it's not our thing. Okay, fine. Live and let live. Let freedom ring, and let sausages race.

Simon, however, apparently has a sausage-racing phobia. As the sausages raced (how often do you see that phrase?), something stirred inside of Simon, then a player for the Pittsburgh Pirates. He witnessed the sausages running, and his hate increased. *I must stop the sausage. The sausage cannot be allowed to race unchecked. The world must be saved from*

In this image from video, Pittsburgh Pirates first baseman Randall Simon, second from left, swats Guido, the Italian sausage (white hat), during the game against the Milwaukee Brewers on Wednesday, July 9, 2003, at Miller Park in Milwaukee. Simon didn't face criminal charges for swatting the young woman in the costume during the popular human sausage race, but he earned an undeniable place in jerkdom. (AP Photo/Fox Sports Net via The Milwaukee Journal Sentinel*)*

errant sausage running freely and wild. The sausage must be annihilated.

As the sausages (sausagees? sausagers?) sprinted past Simon, he leaned over the dugout railing and, utilizing a baseball bat, smacked one of the sausages in the back of its gigantic sausage head. It was like Foreman-Frazier. Down went the sausage! Down went the sausage!

Simon had launched a preemptive sausage attack, except it turns out the sausage had a name: Mandy Block. She was a college student, and after being hit with the bat, she crashed to the ground and scraped her knee.

Now, we admit, when we saw the incident, we laughed hysterically. Then we learned there was a petite young woman behind the sausage, and we suddenly felt horrible for giggling. The incident made national news. Then in a bit of legal ridiculousness, Simon was actually *arrested*. What he did was obnoxious and jerkish, but to arrest the guy was just plain silly. Cops don't have anything better to do than arrest sausage beaters? Simon was arrested for disorderly conduct and suspended by MLB for three games. It was a really stupid move by Simon, but it was also indicative of how our society tends to overreact. You arrest drug dealers and drunk drivers, not sausage abusers.

Simon spent much of his major league career bouncing from team to team and as of late 2008 was with the Newark Bears in New Jersey. Simon also became infamous for something else that was no fault of his own. When John Rocker made his now-historic comments to *Sports Illustrated* in 2000, it was Simon who Rocker referred to as a "fat monkey."

Simon apologized to Block, and his apology was accepted. Fans of the race and the Brewers were eventually able to laugh about the incident. There were even T-shirts printed that read, "Don't whack our wiener!"

Don King

"I found out that someone I believed was my surrogate father, my brother, my blood figure turns out to be the true Uncle Tom, the true nigger, the true sellout. He did more bad to black fighters than any white promoter ever in the history of boxing."
—MIKE TYSON TO ESPN

It's difficult to rely on the words of Mike Tyson who is nuttier than a candy bar, but in this instance, there may be a great deal of truth to his words.

I've met Don King several times. I wanted to give him the benefit of the doubt upon initially speaking with him, but there's little question he's a clown. There is obviously great business acumen underneath the hair and bluster, but you can't see it. King doesn't allow it. That's the odd—and in some ways sad—part. King wants to be taken seriously as a fight manager but who can take him seriously when he behaves the way he does?

There are parts of King's story that are truly, uniquely American. He grew up hard and after dropping out of college ran a highly efficient if not untoward bookmaking machine—an operation that he defended ruthlessly. He shot and killed one man who was trying to rob one of his gambling sites, and he was convicted of manslaughter after beating an employee to death over a matter of $600. It's not many people who can rebound from that kind of beginning and still become, years later, one of the wealthiest men in sports.

King generates many confounding conundrums. He's helped numerous boxers get the opportunity to make millions of dollars, yet other boxers have claimed King defrauded them of just as much money. It seems King taketh and King giveth away. He's been sued by Muhammad Ali, Tim Witherspoon, and Tyson, among other boxers. King has launched his own lawsuits. He sued ESPN and its parent company, Walt Disney Co., for libel over its "SportsCentury" portrayal of him for a staggering $2.5 billion. The lawsuit was like King—all show. The suit was thrown out by a Florida court, and in doing so, the court made an interesting statement about King and his profession. King had argued that ESPN's sources—specifically certain rival boxing promoters— were biased and not credible because they displayed animosity towards King. As Gannett legal writer Barbara Wall chronicled, the court said in the "subterranean world" of contemporary boxing, interaction with some "questionable actors" is to be expected.

Boxing? Questionable actors? Boy, that's putting it mildly. King can't have it both ways. He can't wallow in that at-times-ugly world and then declare himself smudge free. Particularly since there have been boxers who claimed King isn't exactly an angel.

35 Wilt Chamberlain

Maybe we're just jealous. That's what you will say. If the Jerk Council ever had the opportunity to sleep with 20,000 women (or for the women on the council, 20,000 men), we'd jump at it faster than an NFL lineman would leap at a chance to eat a bag of jelly donuts. Maybe back in the day, yes. Maybe. When we were fit and could do pushups. Now we're married, and only our wives and husbands are allowed to see our droopy bellies. We barely let our wives see us unclothed, let alone 20,000 strangers.

Wilt Chamberlain once made the statement that he slept with 20,000 women. That's quite an athletic feat. If true, he deserves the Hall of Fame just for that. We get tired walking up the stairs. 20,000? Is that even biologically possible? At some point, doesn't the *vas deferens* get clogged? Doesn't the prostate gland explode around, say, 9,000 women? For the 20,000 number to be true, Chamberlain would've had to get his sexy on with 1.1 women per day (1.1?) or about eight per week from the time he was a teenager until his death at 63. You'd need a degree from MIT to figure out how many condoms that is (multiply by two, carry the four...holy crap!) Well, from what we've read about Chamberlain, that extraordinary number was damn possible. The man was apparently a machine. One of the most famous quotes about Chamberlain came from his agent Seymour Goldberg who said that, "Some people collect stamps, Wilt collected women."

Chamberlain was a great talent, but he was a ho. There, we said it. He clearly had little respect for women, and perhaps worst of all, Chamberlain's claim played into stereotypes that black men are sexual beasts on the prowl. Tennis great Arthur Ashe lambasted Chamberlain for that exact reason. In his 1993 memoir, Ashe said he didn't believe Chamberlain's claim. "I felt more pity than sorrow for Wilt as his macho accounting backfired on him in the form of a wave of public criticism," Ashe wrote in his autobiography, *Days of Grace*. Ashe added, also speaking of Magic Johnson, "African Americans have spent decades denying that we are sexual primitives by nature, as racists have argued since the days of slavery. These two college-trained black men of international fame and immense personal wealth do their best to reinforce the stereotype."

Chamberlain likely never knew just how embarrassing to him such a claim—no matter the veracity—would become.

Dale Earnhardt Sr.

To some NASCAR fans, Dale Earnhardt is untouchable. He's not supposed to be criticized—ever. To other fans, all these years after his death, he remains a polarizing historical figure. The

---

NBA Big Men

Top Five Greatest NBA Big Men (Most of Whom Likely Never Slept with 20,000 Women...We Think)

5. Bill Walton – Greatest passing big man to ever play the game.

4. Bill Russell – Maybe the greatest winner in sports history.

3. Shaquille O'Neal – Probably could be No. 1, but we're gutless and scared to rank him ahead of two others. Not sure if there's ever been a center with his combination of power and quickness.

2. Wilt Chamberlain – Before Shaq, there was Captain Sex Machine.

1. Kareem Abdul-Jabbar – Was at times simply unstoppable.

Just off the list: Moses Malone, Hakeem Olajuwon, Tim Duncan, Patrick Ewing, George Mikan, and David Robinson.

Dale Earnhardt Sr. leans on the hood of his backup Chevrolet while crew members change out an engine Friday afternoon, February 9, 2001, at the Daytona International Speedway in Daytona Beach, Florida. (AP Photo/ Chris O'Meara)

truth is Earnhardt was a dirty driver. He wasn't just aggressive. He was dirty. He'd rather wreck you if he couldn't pass you. In our opinion, that's dirty. In any language, that's dirty. In any sport, such tactics would be seen as dirty. So why not NASCAR?

He wasn't nicknamed The Intimidator because he was a gentleman on the track. He got that nickname because he drove like a son of a bitch.

Part of that aggression made him the greatest driver ever, but he often got carried away and took out competitors just for the hell of it. In a race at Bristol in 1995, Earnhardt and Terry Labonte were both fighting to win in the final laps, but it was Labonte who had the advantage because of his four fresher tires. In effect, he had the win all but secured. But Earnhardt wasn't done. In one last desperate act, he smacked Labonte, causing Labonte to spin and Earnhardt cruised past him.

Was that cheating or hardcore tactics? If you're an Earnhardt fan you say it was fair, if you're not, or neutral, you say it was dirty. Some fans at the race that day were so angry they booed Earnhardt and gave him the middle finger, among other gestures.

Earnhardt was talented and legendary, but let's not act as if he wasn't one of the greater jerks we've ever seen in sports. He was.

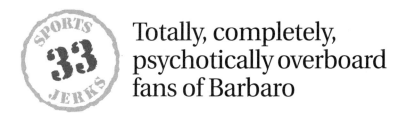

Totally, completely, psychotically overboard fans of Barbaro

We love animals. Dogs are four-legged little gods. Cats are okay, too. One day, we're going to give up burgers and become vegetarians. We want you to know that we love horses, as well. Dogs are heaven-sent, and horses are angels. You need to understand this because as much as we love animals, even we thought fans of Barbaro went completely, totally, and wildly over the top when the horse died.

The best way to chronicle the absurdity of Barbaro fans is by running a portion of a column by CBS national columnist Gregg Doyel who couldn't state more beautifully how big a loser some of those people were "You people scare me," wrote Doyel in December 2006. "You freak me out. And worst of all, there's no way to know who you are. You could be the woman who delivers my mail. The man on the next treadmill. My aunt or my cousin. On the outside you appear normal, but on the inside you're sad and lonely, desperate and degenerate. You're in love with a horse. His name is Barbaro. Your name? I don't want to know your name. I'm still trying to get comfortable with your existence.

"A play has been written about people like you. It's called *Equus*, but you already knew that. For everyone else, *Equus* is Peter Shaffer's 1973 production about a hormonally advanced teenaged boy obsessed with a horse, a boy who satiates his lust by 'sucking the sweat off his god's hairy cheek.' The boy's name is Alan Strang. You people? You lovers of Barbaro? You're strang-e. You're twisted. You have forced the national media to cover Barbaro, the fallen Kentucky Derby winner, as an actual beat. Updates are available daily, sometimes more often than that, if you know where to look. Some reporters cover the Mets. Some cover the White House. Others cover a horse that can barely walk. This is your fault.

"Truth is, Barbaro did become a much more interesting horse after he nearly died, and if he would've had different owners, he'd probably be dead right now. And horse racing might have died with him. Horse racing is a mostly useless sport that gives gamblers a legal excuse to feed their addiction, a sport whose ugly core is disguised by the televised majesty of the Kentucky Derby and Bob Baffert's hair. In recent years the sport has been rocked by drug scandals, with owners doping up their horses to make them run faster, heal faster, etc.

"Along came Barbaro, winner of the 2006 Kentucky Derby by 6½ lengths, the biggest blowout in 60 years. He was a legitimate candidate for the first Triple Crown since Affirmed in 1978, but in the second of those three races he suffered a gruesome injury to his right hind leg. Most times, a horse with an injury like that doesn't leave the track alive. He is put down, euthanized, for humanitarian reasons. Had Barbaro been driven away from Pimlico in a horse hearse, his sport would have joined boxing and men's tennis on life support.

"But Barbaro survived. Horse racing lives to see another year, and thousands of people around the world—I fear it could be millions—have a new hobby: Barbaro stalkers. They're out there, only you don't know who they are. Look at your neighbor. Look at your wife. Someone is sending Barbaro gifts, including a Christmas stocking and a Christmas tree made from edible carrots. Someone is writing him songs and poems. Someone is emailing him."

Barbaro fans responded to Doyel's column with hundreds of angry emails. Let's just say they weren't happy about Doyel's assertions. But Doyel was right. Again, we love animals, but the fans were so overboard it bordered on kookiness.

We've never understood the phenomenon of some who seem to value the life of a strange animal over that of a strange human. I've gotten comments from readers who stated without hesitation how they felt more for Barbaro than a slain American soldier in Iraq. That's a true story. Frightening but true.

 Claude Lemieux

If you're a cannibal, it's likely you're a jerk. That's a fact. It's in the Bill of Rights. Claude Lemieux therefore fits the bill. When Lemieux played with the Montreal Canadiens, he got into a brawl with Calgary's Jim Peplinski. A fight in hockey is like a sunny day in Florida, but this fight was different. While wrestling with Peplinski, the fight-prone Lemieux bit Peplinski on the finger. He bit him. This provided Peplinski with one of the great lines ever, "I didn't know they allowed cannibalism in the NHL."

Lemieux was unbelievably dirty. In a sport where all-out brawls are tolerated—but judiciously mandated—Lemieux seemed to have no problem crossing the line from accepted to cheap. His greatness as a skater and talent was matched by his ferocity and anger on the ice. ESPN named him the most hated player ever in the sport. It's a well-earned title.

One of Lemieux's biggest claims to fame came when he smashed Detroit's Kris Draper into the boards, basically causing Draper's head to explode. After the hit, it looked like someone had stuck a hand grenade in Draper's mouth. Draper needed facial reconstruction and had his jaw, nose, and cheekbone all surgically repaired.

The fact Lemieux was so despised by many players and fans almost overshadows what was a spectacular career. Lemieux was a big-game player who did much of his damage in the postseason. He's also one of only a handful of players to win a championship with three different franchises. We're not certain where he stands in the record books in terms of chomped on fingers.

Tony Stewart

Tony Stewart raced in the Chevy Rock & Roll 400 at Richmond in late 2008. He finished second, extending a winless streak that at the time went back to the 2007 season. Stewart, to say the least, didn't take the loss well. The audio of his, ahem, conversation with crew chief Greg Zipadelli was broadcast

Tony Stewart, left, and crew chief Greg Zipadelli, right, talk in the garage during practice for the NASCAR Sprint Cup Series Coca-Cola 600 auto race at Lowe's Motor Speedway in Concord, North Carolina, on Thursday, May 22, 2008. (AP Photo/Mike McCarn)

publicly and quickly made its way around the Internet. The transcript follows. Remember Stewart's nickname is "Smoke."

Stewart (very sarcastically): "Good job there, guys. We gave another one away today. Great job."

Zipadelli: "10-4. Great attitude there, Smoke. We stalled it a couple times on pit road there and gave up a spot. Remember we win and lose as a team. It was a great effort, okay? Enough of that crap."

Stewart: "The difference is, I got [the places he lost] back."

Cameras caught Stewart tossing equipment around the cabin of his car.

The moment was typical Stewart, who has the maturity of Terrell Owens and the temper of a two-year-old. Like the PGA Tour and its fans, NASCAR and its fans are exemplary at ignoring the faults of their athletes. The auto racing media (like some in the golf media) are complicit in this process. Stewart is rarely taken to task for acting like a petulant child. In 2007 after winning the Allstate 400 at the Brickyard, he said during a nationally televised interview on ESPN, "This one is for everyone in the stands who pull[s] for me and [has] to take all the [expletive] from everyone else." Poor, poor Tony. A millionaire many times over. How does it feel to be so persecuted, Martin Luther Stewart? What was it like to cross the bridge in Selma?

After his cursing on national TV, NASCAR really sunk its teeth into Stewart by fining him $25,000. At that point, he'd earned almost $4 million for that season alone, thus the fine was a drop in a bucket. Before that, Stewart had been fined $10,000 for skipping his media obligations following another race that season.

He has cursed out other drivers, angrily confronted NASCAR officials, kicked aside the tape recorder of a journalist, implied NASCAR caution flags were due to NASCAR rigging the sport like professional wrestling, and said Goodyear "doesn't give a crap" about tire quality. We've probably missed an incident or two. Or three.

Despite all of that, he's still revered as a driver by NASCAR fans and rarely challenged for his behavior. It's that latter fact that might be the biggest travesty of all.

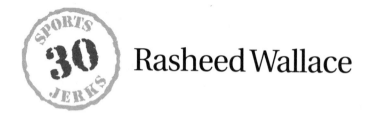

30 Rasheed Wallace

One moment as much as any typified the full-throated jerkiness of Rasheed Wallace. After his team, the Detroit Pistons, lost Game 5 of the Eastern Conference Finals, the hot-tempered Wallace blamed the officials instead of giving the Boston Celtics credit for being the better team. It wasn't just that. It was how Wallace objected to the officiating.

"All that bull[expletive]-ass calls they had out there," Wallace told a group of reporters after the game. "With [game officials] Mike [Callahan] and Kenny [Mauer]—you've all seen that [expletive]. You saw them calls. The cats are flopping all over the floor and they're calling that [expletive]. That [expletive] ain't basketball out there. It's all [expletive] entertainment. You all should know that [expletive]. It's all [expletive] entertainment."

Commissioner David Stern had enough of that (expletive) and fined Wallace's (expletive) $25,000 (expletive) dollars.

When it comes to big men, it's not hyperbole to say that Wallace is one of the most underrated of all time. He's that good. He also possesses a violent temper. That makes him as dangerous as he is talented.

Wallace set an NBA record for technical fouls in 2000 with 41. That's an awful lot of (expletives). It's actually refreshing that players are willing to question authority—particularly NBA officiating, which is sometimes quite shaky. Wallace takes that complaining to an unnecessary plane, however. He questions the most inane calls mainly because he allows that notorious temper to control his logical thinking. Scientists call this manifestation "being a toddler."

Ian Thomsen from *Sports Illustrated* documented a startling confrontation Wallace allegedly had in 2003 with now-disgraced referee Tim Donaghy. Thomsen states that Wallace confronted Donaghy off the court. Wallace allegedly cocked his fist and, when the ref recoiled, said, "You better flinch, you motherf------ punk.... I am going to kick your f------ ass." Wallace denied that he threatened Donaghy with his fist. Maybe he did make the physical threat, maybe he didn't. Wallace, then and now, doesn't get the benefit of the doubt, and for that alleged infraction, the NBA suspended Wallace for seven games. It was the longest suspension ever given by the league for an offense that didn't involve a fight or drug offense. In Game 6 of the 2007 Eastern Conference Finals, he was called for a foul against LeBron James and, in usual Wallace form, objected to what was an obvious foul. Then he was hit with two technical fouls. Incredibly, teammates had to restrain Wallace from going after official Eddie Rush. Remember, this was a crucial Game 6 in the conference finals.

"I just get sick and tired of that cheating out there—all that flopping," Wallace said then.

Wallace likely has several years left in the sport. He's slowing down but only slightly. He has the chance to calm that temper and make his final seasons in professional basketball less about him and his temper. He can alter his legacy, if only slightly. Somehow, however, we don't think he has the maturity. No (expletive) way.

 ## Terrell Owens

B ob Costas did a radio interview with Miami sports journalist Dan Le Batard. No one has defined Terrell Owens better than Costas did on that radio spot. No one.

"I really think that Terrell has some sort of diagnosable personality disorder," Costas said at the time. "I don't know what it is, but it goes beyond garden variety narcissism. I'm not a psychologist, but when you see someone who is often so completely insensitive to the feelings of others and can gratuitously take shots at others, and yet when the slightest

Veteran athor Terrell Owens signs copies of his latest book, T.O.'s Finding Fitness, *at the Sports Museum of America in New York on Tuesday, November 11, 2008. (AP Photo/ Richard Drew)*

thing that touches his sensitivities comes up, he breaks down in tears and [says] 'you don't understand him.' That's infantile. [Owens acts like] 'My feelings are paramount always. The slightest injury to me is a grave injustice. But I can hurl any kind of invective or nonsense at you and be totally insensitive to your feelings and that doesn't matter.' That's how infants view the world."

We wish we'd thought of that. Man, we wish we'd thought of that.

No one throws his former and current teammates under the bus like Terrible Owens. If you created a Hall of Fame for backstabbers, Terrible Owens would be on the first ballot.

He inferred in a 2004 interview with *Playboy* magazine that Jeff Garcia was gay. "Like my boy tells me, 'If it looks like a rat and smells like a rat, by golly, it is a rat,'" Owens said. In the real world, a person's sexual orientation should be irrelevant. In NFL locker rooms, unfortunately, that's not the case. They remain among the most homophobic places in all of sports. Owens knew all of this. His insinuation that Garcia was gay was calculated to do as much damage to Garcia as possible, and the sole reason Owens wanted to injure him was because in Owens' mind, Garcia didn't throw him the ball enough.

That's the crux of Owens' jerkiness. Don't throw him the ball? You're a bad guy. Don't praise him? You're a bad guy. Don't suck his toes or provide a manicure? You're the enemy. He is allowed to verbally attack you, but if you launch a volley that barely brushes him back, Owens treats it like the grandest of assaults. Owens is the epitome of the person who launches insults like grenades and then wilts when insults come his way.

His dances and celebrations don't bother the Jerk Council. He celebrates with stupid little jigs and stunts. So what. Some of them are actually kind of funny.

It's more Owens' treatment of teammates that lands him in prestigious top 30 jerk territory. Owens' treatment of Philadelphia Eagles quarterback Donovan McNabb, for instance, is truly dastardly. We have our own theories why Owens saw McNabb as a threat. It wasn't solely because McNabb was a leader and Owens was jealous. In our opinion—and we're playing therapist like Costas did—Owens was jealous of McNabb's intelligence. Owens isn't all that bright; McNabb is. We think Owens hated that fact more than anything else.

Owens constantly jabbed at McNabb. After Philadelphia's Super Bowl XXXIX loss to New England, Owens told the media that he "wasn't the guy who got tired in the Super Bowl." It was a direct shot at McNabb.

Now what did McNabb ever do to Owens? Nothing. But that's irrelevant in the world of Terrible.

During a holdout with the Eagles, Owens took shots at everyone within his field of vision, literally and figuratively. Owens got into a fight with teammate Hugh Douglas who was a McNabb supporter. Owens pounded team management by calling them classless and again targeted McNabb by saying that if Brett Favre was the quarterback instead of McNabb—who at the time was suffering and playing with a painful sports hernia—the Eagles wouldn't have lost a game up to that point in the year. It was a direct shot at McNabb's toughness. Who can forget Owens doing sit-ups shirtless in his driveway during his dispute with the Eagles? The Eagles first suspended Owens and then released him.

Owens seems to care about his image while simultaneously doing everything possible to sabotage it.

He wrote a children's book in 2006 called *Little T Learns to Share*. Terrell Owens trying to teach kids about sharing.

This is the guy who said, "I love me some me."

You really cannot make this stuff up.

28 Stephon Marbury

In 2005, Stephon Marbury was a married father who had sex with a Madison Square Garden intern in the back of a truck after a night out at a strip club. Romance dead? Nah.

"MSG intern had backseat sex with Stephon Marbury," declared the *New York Daily News*.

Sounds like a movie, *Backseat Confessions with Stephon*.

The details of this SUV romp emerged from the Isiah Thomas sexual harassment lawsuit. It didn't exactly put Marbury in the best of light. The woman intern said in court testimony the sex was consensual. Consensual sex? Good. Consensual sex with a young intern when you're a star basketball player who is married? Well...

Again, we're not judgmental prudes. Sex in a car is fine just as long as everyone is safely buckled up and the car's airbags are temporarily disabled.

It's just that Marbury has sometimes portrayed himself as a good dude when it seems that's not necessarily the case. First, he was a major catalyst for getting Larry Brown fired. Then he publicly feuded with Thomas. It's uncertain who exactly Marbury can get along with other than interns with round bottoms.

27 Kenesaw Mountain Landis

The successor to baseball commissioner Kenesaw Mountain Landis, Happy Chandler, was asked about Landis' stubborn extension of baseball's history of segregation: "For twenty-four years Judge Landis wouldn't let a black man play. I had his records, and I read them, and for twenty-four years Landis consistently blocked any attempts to put blacks and whites together on a big league field." This quote is according to *9 Innings: A Baseball History Reader.*

It also quoted Chandler as saying: "I was named the commissioner in April 1945, and just as soon as I was elected commissioner, two black writers from the *Pittsburgh Courier...*

came down to Washington to see me. They asked me where I stood, and I shook their hands and said, 'I'm for the Four Freedoms, and if a black boy can make it in Okinawa and go to Guadalcanal, he can make it in baseball.'" The story continued, "From the time Chandler made his Four Freedoms statement in April 1945, Branch Rickey took just four months to select the man with the qualifications to break baseball's color barrier. Rickey, however, had been 'making plans' long before then. Rickey had opposed discrimination since the turn of the century when he was the twenty-one-year-old baseball coach of Ohio Wesleyan University…. [R]acism in baseball embarrassed him, but he too knew that as long as Judge Kenesaw Mountain Landis…was commissioner, there was no way he would be able to do anything, and so he kept his thinking to himself as he waited for the day when Landis would step down."

Landis eventually did, and the sport moved forward. A man named Jackie Robinson became the Barack Obama of baseball while Landis was planted in eternal obsolescence.

Good Commissioners

Our Three Favorite Commissioners Ever

3. **Fay Vincent** – Cared more about the game and less about the business of the game.

2. **David Stern** – Maybe the smartest of the commissioners.

1. **Paul Tagliabue** – Underappreciated for his smarts and effectiveness.

Tommy Lasorda

We've chronicled some of the great player and coach outbursts. It'd be neglectful if this outburst from curmudgeonly former Los Angeles Dodgers manager Tommy Lasorda was not noted. It's a classic.

The outburst happened in June 1976. It was prompted after Dave Kingman hit three homers to beat the Dodgers. A reporter simply asked Lasorda a general question about the game. This outrageous question sent Lasorda into a frenzy. Here's the transcript.

Journalist: "Can you give us just a few basic comments about your feelings on the game?"

Lasorda: "Well, naturally I feel bad about losing a ball game like that, there's no way you should lose that ball game. And, it, uh, just doesn't make sense."

Journalist: "What's your opinion of Kingman's performance?"

Lasorda: "What's my opinion of Kingman's performance!? What the fuck do you think is my opinion of it? I think it was fucking horseshit! Put that in, I don't fucking care. Opinion of his performance? Jesus Christ, he beat us with three fucking home runs! What the fuck do you mean, 'What is my opinion of his performance?' How could you ask me a question like that, 'What is my opinion of his performance?' Shit, he hit three home runs! Fuck. I'm fucking pissed off to lose the fucking game. And you ask me my opinion of his performance! Shit. That's a tough question to ask me, isn't it? 'What is my opinion of his performance?'"

Journalist: "Yes, it is. I asked it, and you gave me an answer."

Lasorda: "Well, I didn't give you a good answer because I'm mad, but I mean…"

Journalist: "Well, it wasn't a good question."

Lasorda: "That's a tough question to ask me right now, 'What is my opinion of his performance.' I mean, you want me to tell you what my opinion of his performance is."

Journalist: "You just did."

Lasorda: "That's right. Shit. Guy hits three home runs against us. Shit."

Mr. Lasorda, a question. What's your opinion of a jerk ranking of No. 26?

Quick…duck!

Mike Tyson

There are scientists who believe that for every reality, there is an alternate reality, just as real, just as tangible, invisible, and parallel to the naked eye. In these realities, every possibility and conclusion occurs.

Which means on some alternate timeline, somewhere, Mike Tyson is an astronaut.

He's orbiting the Earth now, in this alternate universe, talking to Houston control, while preparing lab experiments. "Mike," says Houston, "congratulations, you just set a record for the longest spacewalk." Tyson smiles, and in this reality he got braces as a child so his grin is bright and perfect. "It's an honor to walk in the shoes of the great astronauts before me."

Mike Tyson walks out of the courtroom at the Maricopa County Superior Court complex in Mesa, Arizona, on Monday, September 24, 2007. Tyson pleaded guilty to charges of drug possession and driving under the influence stemming from a traffic stop last year as he was leaving a nightclub. Tyson acknowledged to the judge that he had cocaine and was impaired when he was stopped for driving erratically in Scottsdale, Arizona, on December 29. (AP Photo/Tim Hacker)

Really, it's true. In another plane of existence, Mike Tyson is an astronaut. In this reality, however, he is jerk No. 25. Few athletes represent spoiled ability wrapped in pure sociopath while nestled in the armpit of total lunacy as Tyson.

Jerkdom is not just a state of mind; it is a Zen-like place where its inhabitants seem to not arrive through some weird set of circumstances but crave to go. One of the more amazing things about Tyson is that he knows he is a highly flawed human being. He is one of the few jerks who openly acknowledges that he is a jerk. When I briefly interviewed Tyson in 2001, he told me, "People think I'm a nutcase or a bad guy. A lot of times, they're right."

Unlike other jerks such as O.J. Simpson or Kobe Bryant, who are as phony and self-righteous as they are egotists, Tyson does not attempt to deceive the outside world into thinking he is a good guy. To go along with his Zoloft-impervious psyche, there is almost a charming simpleness. He seems to say, "Hi, I'm Mike Tyson and I'm a jerk." Hello, Mike.

The list of Tyson crimes, affronts, and embarrassments is stunning and almost unparalleled. It includes a prison sentence for rape, assault charges, drug charges, felonies on top of warrants on top of drug deals. Well—he might say—at least I haven't killed anyone. True, but he seems to be close to doing that each time he appears in public.

In 2007, Tyson was departing a Scottsdale, Arizona, nightclub when his car almost rammed a police cruiser. It did not take the cast from *CSI* to figure out that Tyson was driving while under the influence of some substance. A greater clue might have been how as officers approached Tyson's vehicle they noticed him wiping a white material off of his face. It wasn't baby powder.

Tyson was arrested for felony drug possession. "He admitted to using...and stated he is an addict and has a problem," according to a police probable cause statement. "Mike admitted to possessing bags of cocaine and said he uses any time he can get his hands on it."

That explains a great deal.

Just a short time earlier, Tyson was in Scottsdale speaking to juveniles in trouble with the law about the dangers of drug and alcohol use. That is a true story. "The irony is he did a great job with these kids—stay away from drugs, don't drink, stay out of trouble," one of the officers said. Words of wisdom from Mike Tyson. Just great.

When leaving prison, the only comment Tyson made to reporters was, "Good morning, Scottsdale." Well, good morning to you.

It is difficult not to look at Tyson with both great humor and epic sadness. The latter emotion is generated more from viewing his wasted potential. Tyson reached the high of knocking out Trevor Berbick in 1986 to become the youngest heavyweight champion at the impossibly young age of 20. One rape conviction and 11 years later, he bit Evander Holyfield's ear. He was once the most feared fighter of his generation, but his inability to control his rage and demons led to Tyson taking not just a plunge deep into jerk territory but to taking one of the most precipitous falls in the history of sports.

And he could have been an astronaut.

 # Ron Artest

I interviewed Ron Artest in July 2007. He was on a cell phone from Africa, and there was a great deal of confusing background noise. Not from the static-filled line, however, but from the mouth of Artest himself.

Noise might not be the right word. During our brief conversation, he was both brilliantly eloquent and semi-coherent. Sometimes in the same sentence. Sometimes in the same breath. When he speaks, Artest's words sound like a combination of riddles, nonsense, parables, and genius.

What do you make of a man who in one moment passionately and sincerely talked of helping the impoverished and in the next giggled over his videotaping of lions humping? (By the way Ron, you didn't have to travel to Africa to see animals having sex. You could've watched that on South Beach.) Artest and a group of

NBA players did something incredibly good that year by engaging in the kind of life-changing adventure and administering of hope we rarely read about our athletes providing. Artest, the players union, a charity group, and the former Secretary of Agriculture teamed up to provide one million pounds of rice and 44 million meals to more than one million residents in and around Nairobi, Kenya. They should be commended for possibly saving thousands of lives and keeping even more people from feeling the sting of starvation.

Artest was in Kenya for more than a week, and there were no reports of riots among Africa's sporting fans. See, Artest is making progress in his life. But this is Ron Artest we're talking about, a man I have come to nickname Episode because he walks through life plopping from one interesting, at times disastrous, episode to the next. The catalyst of a riot one day, a domestic violence charge the next, a charitable act in another moment, an NBA suspension soon after. Episode.

The conversation with Artest alternated between touching, bizarre, intellectual, emotional, and bizarre. And did I mention bizarre? "I taped a cheetah killing a zebra!" Artest exclaimed at one point. "Unbelievable. I watched lions mating. It was wild." Apparently lions don't check into motels in Africa.

He talked about Africa as only Artest could. He remarked about seeing "kids with no shoes on in the middle of the jungle." There was more about lions and their sex lives. He repeated the phrase "you show love, you get love" several times. I'm not sure why. He was clearly startled and humbled by the poverty he witnessed, then displayed some typical athlete aloofness by talking about how everyone in the U.S. needs to visit Africa at least once and how it can "only cost maybe not much, a few thousand dollars, if you want to fly first class" failing to realize that that kind of money is a great deal to the average person.

Then he said this, "Everyone should come here once in their lives. Go to the slums, and it will change how you view your life and the world." You could tell that the hard-ass, troubled man was, for the moment, appreciating the life-altering experiences on a continent far away.

There is a constant battle within Artest, a battle between the good Ron and the bad Ron. The bad Ron seems to be winning, though the good Ron, on occasion, digs in his heels for a fight, which explains Artest doing so much good on that African trip. You constantly wonder and hold your breath for the time when the bad Ron, Mr. Episode, will again emerge. You know he will come screaming out of the shadows. It is only a matter of time.

"Like I tell kids when I speak to them," Artest said at the time, "if you make a mistake, don't be so hard on yourself. Some people make one mistake, some people make 20 mistakes. I'm probably the guy who makes 20 mistakes."

Yes, yes you are.

Even as Artest was helping to do something splendid for potentially a great many people, trouble followed him all the way to Africa. Just as he was in the middle of that trip, the NBA announced Artest would be suspended for seven games as punishment for a no contest plea to misdemeanor domestic violence charges. "The only thing I was really upset about was I was out here," Artest said, "trying to do something good and I had to hear about that news. It was frustrating. But the NBA has a job to do. You just move on."

Artest mentioned something that was unintelligible—this time real phone static was to blame—and then he said, "I'm just being me. People get to see every aspect of Ron Artest's life. Some is good, some is bad, a lot of mistakes. But I'm myself."

"This trip puts things in perspective," he added. "I'm just trying to do something positive with my life." Artest and the NBA players did just that. No question.

What happens next with Artest? He's on a new team, getting a new beginning. Which Artest will win? The one who desires to put the bad times behind him or the devil on the shoulder who makes Artest do crazy and even dangerous things, like being the center of a player riot during an NBA game?

We'll have to wait for the next Episode to find out.

23 Tonya Harding

"I'm not going to make a skeptical out of my boxing career."
—TONYA HARDING TO DAN PATRICK

This book is ridiculously juvenile, if you haven't been able to tell already. The author is a child with a functioning computer and half-functioning brain. One reason why we're children is we laughed hysterically at Harding saying "skeptical" instead of "spectacle." Not that we can break down y = mx + b ourselves, but damn that was funny.

Harding sparring with Patrick is like a fuzzy little bunny taking on a velociraptor. Harding was promoting her new boxing career, but she was no match for a skilled questioner like Patrick. Patrick showed Harding for what she is: a brute who is not very bright.

Harding was a brilliant skater who seemed cursed by bad luck and horrid decision-making. Her most fatal decision was hiring a couple of goons and allegedly conspiring to beat the crap out of Nancy Kerrigan's poor knee ligaments. The plot unfolded in 1994 before the Olympics. Kerrigan was seriously injured but recovered. Meanwhile, Harding's life was irreversibly damaged.

She maintained her innocence regarding plotting the attack but few, if any, believed her then or now.

She basically became a female John Daly. She was considered a joke in her sport and expertly embarked on a post-attack life of stupidity and buffoonery that included the redneck trifurcate: drunkenness, domestic violence, and a sex tape.

She's become a punch line. She's also one of the few jerks for which we feel sympathy. Harding was totally overmatched and overwhelmed by her rise to skating's elite. She wasn't prepared for the spotlight. She became a skeptical—or rather, a spectacle.

# Ben Johnson

When I was covering the NFL for the *New York Times,* there was a great scene that sticks with me to this day. I stood in an NFL locker room with a Pro Bowl player and we were talking about steroids. I told him my belief was that the league's testing program was probably fairly good though it could be better.

"I don't need a testing program, I use the eye test," he told me.

"What are you talking about?" I asked.

He started pointing to teammates in the locker room covertly. He pointed to an extremely muscled-up linebacker. "On the juice," he said, "you can tell by how he's built." He pointed to a less bulky player, "Not him." Then a similarly built player, "Not him." Then he pointed—subtly—to a guy who he thought was using steroids. His point: you can look at a guy and tell instantly. What exactly he looked for is hard to describe, but the best way

Canada's Ben Johnson gives a number one sign after setting a world record for the men's 100 meter and winning a gold medal in the Seoul Summer Olympics on September 24, 1988. Teammate Desai Williams approaches in the background. Olympic officials later stripped Johnson of his gold medal and world record at the games in Seoul after he tested positive for steroids. (AP Photo/Dieter Endlicher)

to state it is if a player is muscular *and* extremely well defined, then some sort of performance-enhancer was involved.

I've spent all this time talking uncomfortably about men's bodies because if this player's notion is correct, it should've been obvious to anyone with working retinas that Ben Johnson was using enough steroids to bulk up Yankee Stadium at full capacity. No human being can be that naturally muscular and defined (there I go talking about the male physique again).

The world was shocked during the 1988 Olympics when it turned out that the world record Johnson set in the 100-meter final was steroid-fueled and Johnson himself a fraud. Johnson is überjerk material not solely because he cheated—hundreds of Olympians have—but because after getting caught he didn't come clean. He lied and for years afterwards stubbornly refused to take total responsibility for what he did. In 2005, he told the *Boston Globe*, "Don't tell me I cheated the system because that's [expletive]," he said. "I didn't get treated fairly by the system. They cast me out, and they were jealous because I turned in the fastest time ever run by a human and it was impossible at the time."

The most disappointed people were Johnson's Canadian countrymen and women. He was hailed as a hero across Canada and just as quickly seen as one of the biggest sporting busts in that country's history.

All anyone ever had to do was take a hard look at Johnson. It would've been obvious what he was doing.

Pacman Jones

It was in the locker room of the Dallas Cowboys following their road win against Green Bay in 2008 where Adam Pacman "Crimetime" Jones showed his true self.

First, go back in time to the summer. Cowboys owner Jerry Jones had taken a dramatic chance in signing Crimetime who'd been arrested six times and involved in 12 instances requiring police intervention after Tennessee drafted him in 2005. Crimetime was on his best behavior all of camp. He was remarkably restrained, almost too much so.

Crimetime's pleasant behavior was, of course, all a ruse. Fast-forward to that locker room after a big Dallas win. The ignorant Jones was back. A journalist (not me) had a simple question for Jones following the game: Would you like to be more involved in special teams play or even involved on offense? Crimetime stared at the reporter and his face looked like someone had just smacked him. "Listen to this chump," Jones said, referring to the reporter.

I watched the scene and was genuinely confused. What the hell was Jones so angry about? The reporter wasn't trying to trick him or stir the pot. It was actually a smart question to ask, and it was posed quite politely.

Pacman then turned to a Cowboys teammate as the writer smiled somewhat awkwardly. "Listen to this chump," Jones said. "What a chump."

"Chump."

Guess Jones thought the guy was a chump. (By the way, who uses the word "chump" any longer? It's very 1970s. Who does Crimetime think he is, Rooster from *Baretta*?)

It wasn't just Crimetime's obnoxious behavior in the locker room that signaled his days at attempting to stay out of trouble were over. Around that time, Pacman got into an altercation with a bodyguard assigned to keep him out of trouble. Please, for one quick moment, digest that bit of news. Pacman got into an altercation with a bodyguard assigned to keep him out of trouble.

That is truly keeping it jerky.

You know someone is a punk when a team assigns a bodyguard not to protect the punk from other people but to protect the punk from himself.

Since Crimetime had already been warned to stay out of trouble, it didn't take long for the NFL to suspend him indefinitely for his most recent incident with the bodyguard.

The total number of incidents in which Pacman has been involved is long and detailed. It would take another jerk book—did someone say sequel?!—to fully discuss them. Among his largest claim to fame is helping to popularize the phrase "making it rain," the process of throwing singles at the feet of exotic dancers. Well, we suppose if you're going to be famous for jerk behavior, you might as well be famous for that.

20 Latrell Sprewell

There is no ego like the athlete ego. If you could harness the athlete ego as a power source, it could light Moscow for decades. It'd be better than nuclear power with no danger of a meltdown. Sprewell embodies this ego in many different ways. In 2004, he was with the Minnesota Timberwolves and embroiled in a bitter contract dispute. The Timberwolves, in Sprewell's final year of a multi-year deal, offered him a $21 million multi-year extension. The average was lower than Sprewell wanted and he fired back at the offer, called it a slap in the face, and made what would become an infamous statement, "I have a family to feed," he told reporters. Sprewell turned the extension down.

The implication was that it was difficult to feed a family on what would've been a salary of $7 million a year. Sprewell is like a handful of jerk athletes who've completely lost touch with reality. How exactly can you not feed a family on $7 million a year? How big is that family? Is Sprewell's family the population of Europe? Is Sprewell supporting all of India?

It was an asinine statement, and what happened next was even more ridiculous. Sprewell rejected offers thinking they weren't rich enough. Eventually, because Sprewell acted like a horse's ass, teams stayed away from him. The irony is that he would need the money. It was reported by the *Milwaukee Journal Sentinel* in May 2008 that Sprewell's home was foreclosed upon because he owed more than $320,000. Before that, according to the newspaper, U.S. Marshalls auctioned his 70-foot yacht valued at $1.5 million for $856,000 after Sprewell couldn't make the $10,322 monthly payments. He also, according to various media reports, owed more than $72,000 in unpaid taxes.

So Sprewell once laughed in the face of a $7 million per season offer but ended up having his home foreclosed upon and his fancy-pants yacht yanked out of his fancy-pants dock. We're not haters. Every American should own a yacht. Yachts are cool. Yet turning down $7 million a year is one of the singularly stupidest acts any athlete has ever done.

Though we all know Sprewell did something else that may have been even dumber.

In 1997, Sprewell also became the symbol for the out of control athlete when he choked his coach, P.J. Carlesimo, during a Golden State Warriors practice. While Carlesimo could be a yelling maniac, all he did was ask Sprewell to pass the basketball more efficiently. Sprewell lost his mind. He was suspended for dozens of games. Though Sprewell was able to slightly rehabilitate his image with the New York Knicks, he'll always be known as the player who choked his coach.

If only Sprewell could have taken Carlesimo for a yacht ride. They could've erased all that tension.

John Rocker

Some jerks are obvious jerks. Some jerks are redneck jerks. John Rocker is both. This is what he told *Sports Illustrated* in 2000 about New York City: "It's the most hectic, nerve-racking city. Imagine having to take the 7 Train to the ballpark, looking like you're riding through Beirut next to some kid with purple hair, next to some queer with AIDS, right next to some dude who just got out of jail for the fourth time, right next to some 20-year-old mom with four kids. It's depressing."

Rocker hit on just about every stereotype there is. The only one missing was that blacks like watermelon and basketball.

The Nobel Laureate continued, "The biggest thing I don't like about New York are the foreigners. You can walk an entire block in Times Square and not hear anybody speaking English. Asians and Koreans and Vietnamese and Indians and Russians and Spanish people and everything up there. How the hell did they get in this country?"

How'd *you* get into this country, dumbass?

It's almost too easy to excoriate Rocker for his jerkiness. It's like harpooning fish in a tank—big, fat, giant, slow-moving fish. One of the things that make it easy is that Rocker never truly seemed apologetic for his full-frontal display of intolerance. Oh sure, he apologized, but he wasn't truly apologetic. There's a difference. We think he apologized to save his butt, not because it was heartfelt. Further proof of this is Rocker's recent "Speak English" campaign, a xenophobic pile of smelly poop, and not so far off from his original rant.

One day Rocker will grow up. It may not occur until he's 70 years old or just before his death, but it will happen. When it does, he's going to look back at his life, and particularly that unfortunate moment in 2000, and say to himself, "What the hell was I thinking?"

Kobe Bryant

We've come to call Kobe Bryant, "Ko-Me Bryant" because of his almost unparalleled selfishness. We think one of the best responses to Ko-Me is the little impromptu rap performed by Bryant's longtime rival Shaquille O'Neal. The rap by O'Neal came after the heavily favored Los Angeles Lakers lost to the Boston Celtics in the NBA Finals. O'Neal took full advantage of the fact that Ko-Me still has yet to win a title without O'Neal. The rap was

Kobe Bryant heads into court at the Justice Center in Eagle, Colorado, on Thursday, May 27, 2004, for a pretrial hearing in his sexual assault case. (AP Photo/Chris Schneider)

precious and quickly became viral because of the signature line, "Kobe, tell me how my ass tastes?"

Now O'Neal isn't always exactly the greatest of teammates. Wrote the *Los Angeles Times* in a blog following the rap: "Seriously, is there anybody in the NBA more willing to throw dudes he used to play with under the bus? First Penny Hardaway. Then Kobe Bryant and Phil Jackson...I'm still willing to buy O'Neal as a good teammate, as enough people have seemed to enjoy sharing roster space with him. But is there a worse EX-TEAMMATE in the league? If I'm Steve Nash or Amare Stoudemire, I've already marked my calendar for a year and a half from now when Shaq's expiring contract gets moved to Charlotte and he starts calling them 'selfish.' It'll be a plum development for Gerald Wallace, however, who'll spend February-April of 2010 suddenly anointed as 'the best small forward I ever played with'...Kobe may not be the easiest teammate in the world to play with, but behavior like this is something he just seems above. Kobe's most notorious public teammate trashing (this summer with Andrew Bynum) was inexcusable, but at least he presumably figured his thoughts were being shared with a couple of random parking lot dudes in private. Shaq doesn't even seem interested in this kind of crap unless there's an audience on hand."

No, Shaq isn't perfect. But Bryant is far worse. It's not even close.

A few members of the Jerk Council have Lakers season tickets, so they hate what we're about to say, but most of us on the council don't mind O'Neal going all Notorious B.I.G. on Bryant since it was Bryant who likely stabbed O'Neal in the back when both were with the Lakers. Bryant, in our opinion, was the main catalyst for O'Neal being shipped off to Miami. There's no question that despite O'Neal saying several times how much he admires Ko-Me as a player, he still feels it was Bryant who sent him East. We think Bryant—and this is our opinion—wanted O'Neal gone so he could have the Lakers spotlight all to himself.

While O'Neal was at times portly and didn't take his physical conditioning seriously—more dunks, less donuts Mr. O'Neal— for the sake of his ego, in our opinion, Bryant pushed for O'Neal's exit prematurely because O'Neal likely had another title in him.

What happened with Ko-Me in 2003 remains debatable. Did he rape a woman in a Colorado hotel room or not? The case for the prosecution fell apart when the alleged victim refused to testify in the trial. The woman eventually filed a lawsuit, and the case was settled out of court. The entire sordid chapter demonstrated what we've believed for some time: Bryant is selfish and a phony.

The rape case provided another reason for O'Neal to hate Ko-Me. The *Los Angeles Times* quoted a police report in which Bryant allegedly stated he "should have done what Shaq does...that

Shaq would pay his women not to say anything." Bryant tossed O'Neal under the bus—allegedly—to the freaking cops.

If true, it doesn't get any more disgustingly selfish than that. "This whole situation is ridiculous," O'Neal told ESPN, responding to the report. "I never hang out with Kobe, I never hung around him. In the seven or eight years we were together, we were never together. So how this guy can think he knows anything about me or my business is funny. And one last thing— I'm not the one buying love. He's the one buying love." O'Neal was referring to how Bryant purchased a diamond ring for his wife following the rape case.

Let's summarize. Ko-Me likely got O'Neal shipped from the Lakers, then when facing a rape case, according to the *Los Angeles Times,* he spoke to police about O'Neal's private life, tossing O'Neal under a police cruiser, not just any old bus. In 2007, Bryant demanded a trade then changed his mind. He's also criticized Mitch Kupchak publicly and teammate Andrew Bynum. So, yes, the nickname of Ko-Me is just about perfect.

17 Barry Bonds

We wrote the following list as Barry Bonds struggled in the summer of 2007 to break the all-time home-run record, and it still applies to one of the nastiest people the sport of baseball has ever seen. These were things we'd rather do than have witnessed Bonds break the record of Hank Aaron, one of the true gentlemen in sports history:

- Count pennies.

- Light our little toe on fire.

- Take a bath in caramel cream Diet Pepsi.

- Hang out for 12 hours with *Star Wars* fans.

- Watch *Road House* eight straight times until I bellow with the cachinnations of a lunatic at Academy Award-worthy dialogue as this:
  > *"You got a name?"*
  > *"Yeah."*
  > *"Well, what is it?"*
  > *"Dalton."*
  > *"Oh my God. I heard of you!"*

- Watch the sequel to *Road House.*

- Watch *Caddyshack II.*

- Read the ramblings of some of the weirdos and bomb throwers on sports message boards.

- Click on the Internet ad that says, "Take this pill and you will have the longest erection in human history."

- Cook possum.

- Hang out with Pacman Jones.

- Or with that walking freight train destined for annihilation, Mike Tyson.

- Sell my baseball card collection.

- Be the slab of roast beef and potatoes at the center of the dinner table once James Gandolfini sat down. Or Tank Johnson.

- Be named "Tank."

- Be Mike Vick. Worse, be his pooch.

- Be one of those bad guys who face the Spartans in the movie *300* and hear, "Spartans, tonight we dine in hell!"

- Get hit with a stun gun. Twice

- Buy O.J. Simpson's book.

- Be sprayed with insecticide.

- Be eaten by a dinosaur, and I don't mean Joan Collins.

- Watch *Shark Week*.

- Be a hamstring in an NFL training camp.

- Watch the X Games.

- Drink green tea.

- Hear Satan exclaim, "I got next."

- Count the grams of fiber we consumed.

You get the point. While there is little question Bonds was subject to massive double standards—people in Congress and the federal government acted as if he was the only steroids user when the entire sport was saturated with performance-enhancing drugs—Bonds was so surly and prided himself so much in treating people around him poorly that he became impossible to root for.

Our biggest problem with Bonds is by extension our biggest problem with many players from the steroid era. Very few of them, almost none of them, ever took responsibility for their acts. Bonds blamed his alleged use on his personal trainer and claimed he thought the trainer was providing flaxseed oil and not steroids. Then Bonds allowed his trainer, once his trainer was busted by the feds, to rot in jail while Bonds roamed free.

Eventually Bonds was indicted on perjury and obstruction of justice charges.

Bonds certainly had an unusual childhood that contributed to his development into an aloof superstar. Bonds is the son of Bobby Bonds, a great talent who fought against harsh racism throughout a productive Major League Baseball career. He passed on those lessons to Barry, and it made Barry extremely guarded about whites specifically and people generally. In his excellent biography, *Love Me, Hate Me: Barry Bonds and the Making of an Antihero*, Jeff Pearlman wrote: "Bobby Bonds had urged his son to be not just guarded, but aloof and antagonistic. The result was a child who craved fame but feared it; who sought friends but turned away those with the potential to grow too close; who needed warmth and affection but refused to show even the slightest bit of vulnerability. Raised in the exclusive white San Francisco suburb of San Carlos, Bonds never knew what it was to blend in with the crowd. He was the black athletic phenomenon with ungodly talent, the kid destined to be a star. He was royalty and was expected to act the part. This does not merely weigh on a youngster. It crushes him."

Some of that is definitely understandable, but at what point is Bonds responsible for being his own person? Again, while Bonds did face double standards on the steroids issue, he was nasty long before then. At some point, you are your own person. There are few if any excuses for behaving the way Bonds did toward other human beings once he became a mature adult.

Pearlman writes of a scene that might describe Bonds as well as any other. Some years ago, Bonds reported to the Prince William Pirates in the Carolina League, a minor league club, walked into manager Ed Ott's office and said, "I'm Barry Bonds, the number one draft pick."

"I'm Ed Ott, and I'm your manager," replied Ott, "and get your [expletive] out that door and don't come in unless you knock!"

Reggie Jackson

W e've heard many stories about Reggie Jackson and how he's treated people. Some of these stories are on the record, while many are off. Few of them put Jackson in a positive light. There are some people who will say that Jackson's bad attitude was calculating and he wasn't as boorish as history has made him out to be. We have our doubts. One of the most infamous stories about Jackson occurred even before he joined the Yankees. The *New York Daily News* chronicled those insane times in New York during what was a fascinating era in baseball. You know a guy is a bit jerkish when one teammate had to work full-time to keep Jackson from getting his ass kicked on a daily basis. "Reggie ought to be glad I was there, because there were guys who wanted to fight him every day, and I wouldn't let them," Paul Blair told the *Daily News*. "My job was to keep the peace. They should've given me another paycheck."

Jackson welcomed himself to the Yankees with a bombastic statement to the then-prestigious *Sport* magazine. At the time, *Sport* had influence and cache and when writer Robert Ward quoted Jackson referring to himself as "the straw that stirs the drink" of the Yankees, it caused a major uproar across baseball. He said this before joining the team. Then the arrogant ass added that one of the star Yankees players, Thurmon Munson, "thinks that he can be the straw that stirs the drink, but he can only stir it bad."

As the *Daily News* wrote: "Three decades later, those words remain a fabled part of Yankee lore, no matter that Jackson has steadfastly maintained that he did not say them—not on the record, and not in such a starkly negative way toward Munson." When one Yankees teammate suggested to Munson that Jackson's remarks had been taken out of context, Munson replied, "For six bleeping pages?"

The biggest problem we have with Jackson is the same one we have with many of our other jerk athletes: They don't take responsibility for their actions or words. How many times do we have to state this? We all make mistakes. The smart person learns from them. Jackson attempted to distance himself from his own words with the eternally gutless mantra, "my quotes were taken out of context." No, they weren't.

Ward says Jackson's reversal and denial of that quote is Jackson trying to save his own butt in the eyes of history. "I never could've made that stuff up in a million years," Ward told the newspaper. "He may be Mr. October, but he's not Mr. Memory."

15 Marion Jones

She denied. Then she denied some more. Then she denied again. Denial, denial, denial. She was so skilled at the denials that you actually believed them. She was so skilled at the denials that she once threatened a lawsuit against anyone who didn't print her version of the truth, then issued another denial. She was excellent at denying the truth and convincing others she was the truth teller even as the evidence mounted against her. No one was as skilled a liar as Marion Jones. Not Bill Clinton, not Rafael Palmeiro, not Jim Carrey's character in *Liar Liar*.

Give 'em back: Marion Jones holds up her five Olympic medals for track and field events outside the Opera House in Sydney, Australia, in this October 1, 2000, photo. The results were annulled in 2004. (AP Photo)

Jones is a perfect example of how the cover-up can be worse than the crime. Indeed, her performance-enhanced bravado was some of the greatest bluffing since the World Series of Poker. Jones actually dared people to accuse her and threatened potential accusers with legal action. It was all a wonderfully choreographed bluff.

In her 2004 autobiography, *Marion Jones: Life in the Fast Lane*, she wrote on page 173 in large red letters: "I HAVE ALWAYS BEEN UNEQUIVOCAL IN MY OPINION: I AM AGAINST PERFORMANCE ENHANCING DRUGS. I HAVE NEVER TAKEN THEM AND I NEVER WILL TAKE THEM."

That, of course, was false. Jones would later admit that she lied to federal investigators about her use of banned drugs from 1999 to 2001. Jones was another performance enhancer in the world of track and field. There are more dopers in track than there are six packs in John Daly's refrigerator.

The suspicions surrounding Jones in 2001 were understandable. Her husband at the time, C.J. Hunter, a shot putter, tested positive for nandrolone four times the year before. Many Jerk Council members are married and we don't do laundry without first checking with the significant other, let alone steroids.

Clue two: When Hunter gave his press conference to talk about his positive test, he was flanked by Victor Conte who was identified as Hunter's "nutritionist." Ding, ding, ding! Red alert! If Conte is in the room, then Mr. Steroid must be nearby.

Jones testified before a federal grand jury investigating BALCO and still denied any involvement with steroids. The U.S. Anti-Doping Agency threatened to bar her from competing in the Athens Olympics and not only did Jones fail to keep a low profile, she threatened to sue the agency. When Conte turned on Jones and said he provided her with a variety of banned substances, Jones again denied any wrongdoing, and in an amazing case of bravado, sued Conte for defamation of character all the while knowing she was guilty. Jones certainly did have a chemically enhanced pair (of ovaries) on her.

In the end, the unsurprising truth was that Jones had been doping all along. The International Olympic Committee took back her gold medals and banned her from future games. "People ask me…if her achievements are tainted," Conte told *USA Today*. "In my opinion, the overwhelming majority of athletes Marion competed against in 2000 were also using performance-enhancing substances. So I believe she deserves the medals. We need to change the focus and put the spotlight upon Olympic governing body officials, owners of pro sports teams and players' union representatives—those that control the money in elite sport."

Conte is correct about one thing. It's likely that so much cheating goes on in track and field that Jones probably did compete against many cheaters. That's no excuse. It's also no excuse just how much she fooled so many loyal fans who took her proclamations of truth as gospel only to be deceived in the end.

This is the frightening part. Many times Jones was tested for performance enhancers while she was using them, and many times she passed the tests. "I'm not exactly happy to know that I tested her many times and she passed," Dr. Don Catlin, who was in charge of the UCLA Olympic Analytical Lab from 1982 to 2007, said to *USA Today*. "We're never happy to know that we missed people because we miss people all the time. It's bittersweet because she always passed, but it's sweet because she finally confessed. The message is simple: Crime doesn't pay."

14   Mark McGwire

On an extraordinary day, an extraordinary hitter, Mark McGwire, wearing a dark suit and lime green tie, his hair and memory both apparently equally thin, sat before a Congressional hearing and systematically, point by point, almost tear by tear, single-handedly destroyed his legacy.

In 2005, the House Government Reform Committee was taking a hard look at baseball's remarkably flawed steroid testing

....

Steroids?

Five Biggest Excuses Players Use After Testing Positive for Steroids

5. **"I kissed a woman wearing nandrolone lipstick."**

4. **"Someone slipped steroids in my coffee."**

3. **"I have a twin brother. It was really my brother that tested positive, not me."**

2. **"HGH? I thought I took PCP."**

1. **"My testicles are naturally this small."**

....

program. One of the most anticipated witnesses was McGwire. He had the chance to declare he had never used steroids. Instead, a shrunken McGwire repeatedly deflected questions from committee members about his alleged steroid use. It was basically an admission of guilt; at least, that's how much of the American public took it. How could they not?

McGwire's non-testimony will go down as one of the worst and saddest moments in the sport's history.

McGwire was, to be blunt, gutless. He hid behind lawyers. "Asking me or any other player to answer questions about who took steroids in front of television cameras," McGwire testified, "will not solve the problem...My lawyers have advised me that I cannot answer these questions without jeopardizing my friends, my family, and myself. I intend to follow their advice."

"I'm not here to discuss the past," was a McGwire mantra. The phrase became a joke across the sports world.

Then McGwire disappeared from public life. He fell off the face of the planet. He ran. The man who was Paul Bunyan suddenly became small both physically and metaphorically.

Manny Ramirez

We thought the best way to begin our little fireside chat about Manny Ramirez was run a portion—just a smidge—of something that can best be described as Manny Watch. It's the *Boston Globe*'s running scorecard of all the überknuckleheadedness of Ramirez. This is only a portion, and the total tally is incredible. Actually, it's stunning:

- **September 2001:** Missed last game of the year for "personal reasons." In that game, the Red Sox honored Cal Ripken, which was Ripken's last game at Fenway Park.

- **December 2001:** The Red Sox decide to build a separate room for media interviews because Ramirez says he's uncomfortable in the locker room. Poor guy.

- **May 2002:** Lost his $15,000 diamond earring while sliding into third base.

- **September 2002:** Asks for song "Good Times (I Get High)" by Styles P to be played over the stadium loudspeaker when he bats. The song is an ode to drug use and full of obscene lyrics. Like idiots, the Red Sox oblige.

- **September 2002:** Hits a homer. Then in ensuing at-bat, hits a ground ball and doesn't leave the batter's box. Nice effort.

Manny Ramirez hangs his head as he leaves the batter's box after striking out during the ninth inning of a game against the Baltimore Orioles on Wednesday, May 17, 2006, in Baltimore. (The Orioles won 4–3.) (AP Photo/Chris Gardner)

- **August 2003:** Says he would like to play for the Yankees. There is no greater insult to a Red Sox fan than a Red Sox player lusting for the Yankees.

- **August 2003:** This is one of our favorites. Ramirez says he's too sick to play in a big series against the Yankees. But he's seen in a bar, hanging out with a friend who plays on the Yankees.

- **Fall 2003:** Refuses to pinch hit and is benched for the next game.

- **July 2005:** Takes the day off despite manager Terry Francona declaring Ramirez was needed. Oh, just Manny being...never mind.

- **August 2005:** Doesn't hustle to first and is thrown out.

- **September 2005:** Doesn't hustle to first and is thrown out. (This could actually probably be repeated several hundred times).

- **October 2005:** Stories appear in the media, stating Ramirez demanded to be traded and would boycott spring training if he wasn't.

- **July 2006:** Commissioner Bud Selig is agitated about Ramirez not coming to Pittsburgh for the All-Star Game because of a tender knee despite being the AL's leading vote-getter. "Maybe I'm old-fashioned, but if you are voted on the team, it's a privilege," Selig told the media. "You ought to be here. He's the only person who did not participate this year. Everybody else has been here and has been terrific." Reward the fans for voting him to the All-Star Game by showing up? Why so demanding, commissioner?

- **September 2006:** Missed 22 of 30 games late in the year with alleged patellar tendonitis.

- **June 2008:** Gets into a dugout scuffle with Kevin Youkilis. Oh, just Manny being…never mind.

- **June 2008:** Shoves a 60-year-old traveling secretary to the ground.

- **July 2008:** Talks on a cell phone during a pitching change.

- **July 2008:** Sits out pivotal game against the Yankees, infuriating the Red Sox.

- **July 2008:** Tells ESPN, "The Red Sox don't deserve a player like me." They trade him to Los Angeles.

Ramirez isn't a woman beater. He doesn't have a long list of felonies. He's not a drunk. That's what it has come to these days. We praise athletes who don't get arrested. He is, however, someone who wastes his abilities and takes them for granted. In some ways, that's one of the greatest sins you can commit in sports.

12 Reggie Bush

Reggie Bush is not your classic jerk. There's no warrant out for his arrest. No HGH in his system. No woman-beating on his record. In fact, there's no record. He's a fairly swell fellow except for the fact that as of late 2008, the USC football program remained in serious danger of receiving significant penalties from the NCAA because of Bush's alleged greed.

We're extremely liberal when it comes to college kids and sports. Big-time college sports are basically the minor leagues for the pros except the kids aren't officially paid salaries. They should be. They should be paid lots of cash because they earn billions of dollars in revenues for the schools. And please do not talk about how they earn scholarship money. Those funds are paltry compared to the cash they bring to schools.

This is all true.

The problem we have with Bush—and why he earns such supreme jerk honors—is that if the allegations are true (and he denies them), boy did Bush get greedy. He took the notion of players deserving to be paid to an entirely different level.

Yahoo! Sports (never forget the exclamation point!) reported in 2006 that Bush and his family were allegedly given $280,000 in cash, rent, and gifts while he was at USC. If the allegations are accurate, that's beyond piggish. That's historic greed. That's the kind of greed that movies are made about.

The NCAA has the authority not only to sanction USC for Bush's alleged violations, but they should also take away his Heisman Trophy. We're not sure the NCAA will ever do either. The NCAA tends to be a tad spineless in these areas. What's not in question is that Bush probably—and this is our opinion—went too far in accepting gifts. The monies he's alleged to have received from brokers and agents are in amounts we'd never heard before. The NCAA needs to take some sort of stance against this type of alleged excess. What's next? Some agent giving a college player a small country?

11 Dave Bliss

Dave Bliss can be heard on a tape plotting to call one of his murdered players a drug dealer. In part, Bliss is heard saying, "Our whole thing right now, we can get out of this. Reasonable doubt is there's nobody right now that can say we paid Pat Dennehy because he's dead. So what we need to do is create reasonable doubt." Remember, this is *a coach* talking this way. *A coach.* And his way of trying to create reasonable doubt was attempting to plant false rumors that the murdered player was a drug dealer.

Bliss is a man who could easily be the top-dog jerk. His story is as unbelievable as it is disgusting. It starts with the disappearance and murder of Baylor University basketball player

Patrick Dennehy. He was killed during an argument by Baylor teammate Carlton Dotson. After the death, Dotson pled guilty to the murder and was sentenced to 35 years in jail. That is a sad enough tale, but it's only half of the story. The other half centers on Bliss, who will go down as one of greatest scoundrels in sports history.

Bliss' attempt to blame a murder victim begins with Bliss committing massive NCAA violations. The key violations involved partial payment of Dennehy's tuition. This was the crux of Bliss's frightening thought process. As investigators explored the accusations that Dennehy had received illicit payments from Bliss, it was Bliss who instructed players and coaches to tell investigators that Dennehy got the extra money not from Bliss but from selling drugs. It was a disgusting tactic.

The irony is that Bliss' cowardice would never have been known had it not been for a hero named Abar Rouse, an assistant on the Baylor team who recorded Bliss' comments. Another irony: despite doing the right thing, Rouse is now blackballed in the coaching profession because he's seen as a traitor—which illustrates the occasional group-think stupidity of the coaching profession.

"I'm the head coach, and I'm accountable for everything that goes on in my program," Bliss told the media at the time. "I accept that responsibility. I intend to cooperate fully as the inquiry continues. I'll do whatever I can to make things right."

That was a lie. Bliss never intended to do anything of the sort. As he was saying that to the media, he was plotting to frame Dennehy as a drug dealer.

It's difficult to tell what would motivate Bliss to call a murdered man, a good man, a drug dealer. Just to save his skin from NCAA investigators? Is that it? You try to destroy your murdered player's reputation just to avoid sanctions? Is that how little Bliss thinks of human life?

This is the scary part. After the Baylor scandal, Bliss got a job coaching in the Continental Basketball Association. Why anyone would ever hire Bliss is beyond us. He doesn't seem fit to run a lemonade stand.

Of the 100 jerks (plus the runner-ups), only two are personal. This is one of the two, but that still doesn't lessen Robert Irsay's place in scoundrel history. I was born in Washington, D.C., and raised in a Maryland suburb. I went to high school in Baltimore, a small Catholic school where I learned about the Bible and how to smoke pot. So I claim both D.C. and Baltimore as my cities. I'm passionate about both. Baltimore remains one of the most underrated cities in the country when it comes to passionate sports fans. Baltimore Colts football was a dire necessity to your average Baltimoron, like oxygen and Pop Tarts. I was one of the few people who was both a Washington Redskins and Baltimore Colts fan. I once took a Colts jersey and a Redskins jersey, cut them in half, then made a single jersey composed of half of the Redskins leftover and half of the Colts jersey. I was a psycho. But I loved my Colts.

When Irsay moved the team, it was like a hammer hitting you in the face. It wasn't just that he moved the team, it was *how* he moved the team. If you were a Baltimoron, you literally woke up one morning in 1984 and your team was gone. Goodbye. It wasn't like the Cleveland Browns or other franchises. There was no long buildup and lengthy negotiations. Those other teams had some sort of warning. Colts fans didn't.

Irsay literally crept out of the city in the middle of the night like a coward.

I remember people I went to high school with as well as other friends who literally cried. I mean, these people were cops and soldiers and tough guys. They cried. To some of these men—and I'm not kidding—the Colts leaving was like their wives bolting town with the kids.

What makes Colts fans angry to this day—the anger is passed down from parent to child—is Irsay's declaration. Declaration wasn't the word; Irsay made a promise to the city of Baltimore. Irsay told the media during a press conference there was no chance the Colts were leaving Baltimore, which is why Colts fans were so shocked when they later did—people actually believed Irsay.

Since Irsay thought the city of Baltimore might seize his team (it's highly debatable and unlikely the city could've done that) he made the move to Indianapolis as a sort of preemptive strike (or at least that's what Irsay wanted the public to believe). The truth is, Irsay made a money grab. Indianapolis offered him a lot of cash, and he took it. That's it. End of story.

So during the early morning hours, under the cover of darkness, Irsay brought a contingent of Mayflower moving fans to the Colts facility in Owings Mills, packed up the team, and moved them. No one truly knew what had happened until dawn. The city was shocked and angry.

Wrote *Sports Illustrated* two years after the move: "Baltimore Mayor William Donald Schaefer, who was recently elected governor of Maryland, once described Irsay as 'one of the most interesting men I've ever met.' That is a fine example of euphemism. Schaefer had publicly been Irsay's defender until late on the night of March 28, 1984, when he heard the news over the radio that the Colts were packing up to leave. His spokesperson, Pat Bernstein, was recently asked if Schaefer had gotten over the manner in which Irsay had spirited the club out of town in the dead of night without the courtesy of a phone call. 'I don't think you ever get over betrayal like that,' she said. 'The presumption was always that the mayor was dealing with somebody who had some scruples. But when [Irsay] told you one thing and turned around and did exactly the opposite, you got the feeling that you weren't dealing with an equal partner.'"

So not even the mayor knew what Irsay was planning. The mayor found out the same way the rest of us did—from the media.

Colts fans called it "The Move," which it is aptly named. I remember other Colts fans referring to it as "The Colts Bolt."

These quotes from *Sports Illustrated* are priceless and really say a lot about Irsay. Wrote the magazine: "Bert Jones, the man who quarterbacked the Colts to their three winning seasons under Irsay, will only paraphrase a quote he originally gave to *The Sun* in Baltimore when asked about Irsay: 'He lied and he cheated and he was rude and he was crude and he was Bob Irsay.' Then Jones added, 'He doesn't have any morals. It's a sad state for the NFL to be associated with him, but beyond that I've removed him from my mind.' Mike McCormack, who coached the Colts in the 1980 and '81 seasons, says, 'Those were the two most unpleasant years of my life and I really don't care to comment further on it.' Irsay's mother, Elaine, is 84 years old and in failing health. Reached by phone at her home in Rolling Meadows, Ill., Mrs. Irsay, who still has a rich Hungarian accent, said, 'He's a devil on earth, that one.' Every few seconds she paused for breath, her voice rising at the start of each thought, then quickly tiring. 'He stole all our money and said goodbye. He don't care for me. I don't even see him for 35 years. My husband, Charles, sent him to college. I made his wedding. Five thousand dollars, it cost

Worst Owners

The Top Five Worst Owners in Sports History

5. Leon Hess, former owner of the New York Jets – Terrible.

4. William Clay Ford, owner of the Detroit Lions – Fiddled while Matt Millen burned down the Lions.

3. Bill Wirtz – Owned the Chicago Blackhawks and was notorious for his frugality.

2. James Dolan – Fiddles while the Knicks burn.

1. Robert Irsay – The Mayflower moving vans in the middle of the night were truly a nice touch.

us. When my husband got sick and got the heart attack, he [Bob] took advantage. He was no good,' she said. 'He was a bad boy. I don't want to talk about him.'"

When your own mother says that about you, you really are a supreme jerk. (Dear Mom: Please don't rip me if the media comes a-calling. Love you!)

Irsay signed a 20-year lease with Indianapolis. To them, Irsay was a hero. To us, he was a disgrace. When Irsay died on January 14, 1997, at the age of 73, there were fans of the Colts who celebrated.

"Locker room tantrums. Bad trades. Tight-fisted ways," wrote one newspaper in its Irsay obituary. "There were many stories about Irsay's 12 years as owner of the Baltimore Colts, and no shortage of former players and coaches—even relatives—willing to speak ill of the man." No shortage indeed.

One man's (or woman's) hero is sometimes another man's (or woman's) goat. Indy loved Irsay and Baltimore despised him the same way Baltimore loved Art Modell and Cleveland felt the opposite. Baltimorons can't complain about having their team stolen when they stole another city's.

But we do have the right to complain about Irsay. And we do. And we will forever, and I mean, forever.

 Bob Knight

ESPN compiled its list of the top 10 Bob Knight sound bites. All they did was take portions of Knight's press conferences and splice them together. It was so simple yet so entertaining. Knight is so atrociously foul-mouthed in a public setting it's stunning. We love a little foul language ourselves. You should hear the treasurer on the Jerk Council. Whew. F-bomb this, curse word that. Yet no one—and we mean no one—defines foul-mouthed turd bully like Bob Knight.

Knight isn't the worst human being ever. No. Those types of distinctions are for, well, mass murderers. Knight is, however, not a very good person. Great coach, bad guy. Wikipedia has compiled a list of Knight transgressions, and it's an eye-opening read when you see everything Knight has done. We've confirmed the accuracy of this list with multiple media sources. Your eyes may need to be partially covered:

1. In 1979, Knight was arrested for assaulting a police officer during the Pan American Games in Puerto Rico. Knight was angry that a practice gym wasn't open. Knight was later convicted in a Puerto Rican court. However, the

Texas Tech coach Bob Knight yells during the second half against Charlotte in their NCAA men's basketball championship first-round game on Thursday, March 18, 2004, in Buffalo, New York.

charges were later dropped when the Indiana governor refused to cooperate in extraditing Knight to the island commonwealth. That was likely one of the first moments when Knight knew he could get away with anything because he was a basketball coach. After all, he punched a law enforcement officer and was never punished for it. Imagine the reaction in this country if a Puerto Rican coach punched an American police officer and then Puerto Rico refused to turn over the offender. People here would demand we send in the Marines.

2. Knight threw a chair across the court to protest a referee's call during a game against Purdue. He was suspended for one game and received two years' probation from the Big Ten Conference.

3. In one of the most offensive comments ever made by a sports figure, Knight told Connie Chung in 1988, "I think that if rape is inevitable, relax and enjoy it." We think if a stellar jerk ranking is inevitable, relax and enjoy it.

4. During a game, Knight kicked a chair that his own son was sitting in. Pat Knight played for his father.

5. At times Knight is truly detestable. It's one thing to bully your players. It's another to treat college administrators and NCAA officials with such abusive disdain. During one NCAA tournament, Knight verbally abused an NCAA official who mistakenly didn't know that Emperor Knight was going to make a press conference appearance.

"You've only got two people that are going to tell you I'm not going to be here," Knight yelled at the official. "One is our [sports information director], and the other is me. Who the hell told you I wasn't going to be here? I'd like to know. Do you have any idea who it was? Who? They were from Indiana, right? No, they weren't from Indiana, and you didn't get it from anybody from Indiana, did you? No, I—I'll handle this the way I want to handle it now that I'm here. You [expletive] it up to begin with. Now just sit there or leave. I don't give a [expletive] what you do. Now, back to the game." The whole scene was typical Knight.

6. Knight's serial verbal abuse tendencies led to him getting canned at Indiana, and he finished his career at Texas Tech. Knight outdid himself when he got into a verbal altercation with the chancellor of the school at a supermarket. How'd that argument go exactly?

Texas Tech Chancellor David Smith: "Wow, this spinach sure is fresh, huh coach Knight?"

Knight: "[expletive] you and your [expletive] spinach."

Actually, it went like this, according to Lubbockonline. com, which wrote: "Smith went over to the salad bar to talk to the coach. Knight flew into a rage, accusing Smith of being a liar and saying that there had been nothing wrong with his demeanor this year. At that point, Smith backed away and turned to leave the area. Knight continued to follow Smith, who stopped and told Knight that he was chancellor of the university and deserved more respect from him."

The lesson—never bother Knight at the salad bar. If you do, he might strangle you with an artichoke.

7. Video emerged in 2006 of Knight allegedly hitting one of his players, Michael Prince, under the chin. Prince said Knight didn't hit him, but at this point, does Knight get the benefit of the doubt?

8. In 2007, a Texas man said Knight fired a shotgun in his direction after he confronted Knight and a friend of Knight's for hunting too near the man's house. Bob Knight and a shotgun. What could go wrong?

Are there good things Knight does? He graduated his players. That's true. But that doesn't excuse or exclude what are enough boorish incidents to fill several books. Several curse-filled books.

Brett Favre

The story below was written by me for CBSSports.com. It's tongue-in-cheek and perfectly describes The Selfish One. It was written after Brett Favre made a comeback with the New York Jets just months after retiring:

> Hello, everyone. Brett Favre here.
>
> You ask: Why come back? Good question.
>
> Here's the answer. Because I'm Brett Lorenzo Favre, and you're not. That's why.
>
> Clear everything up for you?
>
> If my comeback does anything it should finally make all of you suckers realize that I love me some me.
>
> I'm more Terrell than Terrell.
>
> "Like your style, Brett," said Chad Johnson.
>
> Thank you, Ocho. I learned from the best, my brotha.
>
> Did you see me mentioned on ESPN several thousand times in a 13-minute span? Did you see? They set the record for blatant pandering to me, previously held by John Madden.
>
> I need my own network. Brett TV sounds good.
>
> People say the sports world is utterly sick of me. False. It's not true that fans throw up in their mouths when they hear my regal name.
>
> Just Googled myself an hour ago. They're talking about me all over those fancy Internets website thingies. Bored of me? People can't get enough.

New York Jets quarterback Brett Favre listens to a question at a New York City Hall news conference, Friday, August 8, 2008. The Jets acquired Favre from the Green Bay Packers for a conditional draft pick. (AP Photo/ Richard Drew)

So what if I'm really a selfish, egotistical, franchise-wrecking rube who gives new meaning to the word diva. Who cares? Everyone is talking about me again. Me, me, me.

Because I'm Brett Lorenzo Favre, and you're not.

My old teammate Mark "Hot Tub" Chmura, referring to me, once said, "People who don't think that it's all about him are fooling themselves."

Have to say ol' Hot Tub nailed that one about the Brettinator. But if I retire, how will announcers constantly talk about my gunslinger mentality?

And what about Aaron Rodgers, you ask? What about him? He's my apprentice in perpetuity.

His feelings? This is football, people. Brett Favre isn't Dr. Phil. Brett Favre is Brett Favre is Brett Favre.

Aaron can suck on a lemon. So can Dr. Phil.

When I'm playing for the Tampa Bay Buccaneers next season, Aaron will still be my apprentice in perpetuity.

For Christmas I'm sending him a clipboard just so he feels at home.

Knock, knock. (Who's there?) Aaron? (Aaron who?) Aaron where's your clipboard?

Damn I'm funny. The best part about being me? Playing Jedi mind tricks with GM Ted Thompson. I'm coming back, not coming back. Coming back, not coming back. Pulled the old okey doke on Teddy boy.

Then Teddy announced to the world that I would be a backup to my apprentice in perpetuity.

"Quite frankly, it's a little gut-wrenching as an organization to go through it..." I read Thompson say. "This stuff hurts a lot of people. I mean, it hurts. I'm not talking about physically hurting, but the sensitivity. We understand where the fans are coming from. This is a hot-button issue that surpasses anything I've ever gone through."

Boo freaking hoo, crybaby. And we'll see who wins this fight, Teddy boy.

One snap of my Hall of Fame fingers and I can have 20,000 cheeseheads pepper you with slices of very sharp cheddar. Preferably the organic kind.

All this time I've fooled the cheeseheads into believing I'm just a humble good old boy when actually I'm Gordon Gecko in shoulder pads.

Because I'm Brett Lorenzo Favre, and you're not.

Do you finally understand that?"

Again, that was written tongue-in-cheek, but it wasn't so far off. The worst part about Favre leaving the Packers was that he blamed the Packers. Favre had retired and then unretired. The Packers had moved on. Just because Favre changed his mind—at

the last minute—doesn't mean the Packers have to oblige. Favre
thinking anything else is just pure athlete ego.

Favre has always been a stealth T.O. He's always been one of
the most self-centered athletes in NFL history. It was just cloaked
by his golly-gee, aw-shucks, gosh-darn demeanor, which was
never authentic. Favre has always been a diva. No more, no less.

Pete Rose

The big problem with Pete Rose has always been that he
denied betting on baseball when anyone with standard
brain chemistry knows he did. Part of Rose's long denial before
his sudden admission to gambling is understandable. Rose knew
the massive damage that such an admission would cause to his
legacy and he knew there was a possible, if not probable, chance
he'd never be reinstated to baseball.

"The issue is protecting the game, not protecting Mr. Rose
and his reputation," former baseball investigator John Dowd
told National Public Radio. "That's the judgment that's been
made on anyone who's ever bet on the game, and I think we
ought to honor that. In my judgment, I don't think there are
any circumstances that justify his return to the game.... If you
let Rose back in, then the message to anyone who gambles and
gambles on the game is that if you throw enough of a public
relations tantrum and admit that you did it, then you ought to
be back in the game."

As Dowd noted, and NPR wrote on its website, no one who's
been declared permanently ineligible to participate in baseball

Former Cincinnati Reds manager Pete Rose, left, goes over alleged gambling sheets with Phil Donahue during taping of the Donahue Show at the NBC studios in Burbank, California, on Wednesday, November 9, 1989. (AP Photo/Bob Galbraith)

has ever been readmitted. Commissioner Selig is "coming up against a great deal of powerful history on a rule that has been time and again demonstrated to prevent the corruption of the game," Dowd explained.

The force of the rule is "remarkable" Dowd says. When Bart Giamatti banned Rose, Dowd remembers that the former commissioner "got calls from ballplayers all over the country" thanking him for "protecting the rule because they obey it. It's posted right on the clubhouse door, and they get reminded every spring what it is because experience has taught us that [gambling] really does undermine the game and it can't be ignored."

If Rose, after being busted for gambling on baseball, had come clean immediately and publicly thrown himself at the mercy of baseball and fans, he might've been reinstated by now. The problem was Rose himself. The same personality aspects that made Rose a great player also made him unwilling to look in the mirror and accept who he really was—a man who gambled on baseball.

Rose's image completely transformed following his playing career. He went from Charlie Hustle to Charlie Con. He lied for decades about his gambling. It was worse than that. At one point, he sued the commissioner's office, alleging that his case had been prejudged. From the late 1980s until 2004, Rose repeated his denials. His interview with the relentless television and radio journalist Jim Gray before Game 2 of the 1999 World Series typified Rose's stubborn refusal to admit the truth.

> Jim Gray: "Pete, now let me ask you. It seems as though there is an opening, the American public is very forgiving. Are you willing to show contrition [and] admit that you bet on baseball and make some sort of apology to that effect?"
>
> Pete Rose: "Not at all, Jim. I'm not going to admit to something that didn't happen. I know you're getting tired of hearing me say that. But I appreciate the ovation. I appreciate the American fans voting me on the All-Century Team. I'm just a small part of a big deal tonight."
>
> Gray: "With the overwhelming evidence in that report, why not make that step...."
>
> Rose: "No. This is too much of a festive night to worry about that because I don't know what evidence you're talking about. I mean, show it to me...."
>
> Gray: "Pete, those who will hear this tonight will say you have been your own worst enemy and continue to be. How do you respond to that?"
>
> Rose: "In what way are you talking about?"
>
> Gray: "By not acknowledging what seems to be overwhelming evidence."

Rose: "Yeah, I'm surprised you're bombarding me like this. I mean I'm doing an interview with you on a great night, a great occasion, a great ovation. Everybody seems to be in a good mood. And you're bringing up something that happened 10 years ago…. This is a prosecutor's brief, not an interview, and I'm very surprised at you."

Gray was perfectly within his right to ask Rose at that time, and anyone who thinks otherwise is foolish. Pay close attention to Rose's words, "I'm not going to admit to something that didn't happen." This is in sharp contrast to just a short few years later when Rose told Dan Patrick, "I bet on my team every night. I didn't bet on my team four nights a week. I bet on my team to win every night because I loved my team, I believed in my team. I did everything in my power every night to win that game." It was finally an admission even if it was a manipulative one.

Rose is a classic jerk but also a sad case. He's still not in the Hall of Fame. The Hall of Fame without Rose is like Alaska without Sarah Palin. Yet it's also understandable why Rose is banned. It's not just that he bet on baseball. It's that for decades, he lied about it. He was, in effect, a coward, and when would you think anyone would ever say that about Rose?

John Daly

One day in 2008, John Daly went out for a night of drinking at Hooters. Somehow all of that sounds perfectly normal. John Daly…lots of drinking…Hooters. The only thing missing

John Daly was taken into custody October 26, 2008, by Winston-Salem police after he was found drunk outside a Hooters restaurant in Winston-Salem, North Carolina.

from that sentence are the words "ex-wife" and "Daly missed another cut."

So Daly goes out to drink and, according to Winston-Salem police, got so plastered and sloppy drunk that they said he was, according to a police report, "extremely intoxicated and uncooperative." They hauled Daly off to jail and put him in an orange jumpsuit, size XXXXXL. The picture of Daly wearing his shiny new jumpsuit made headlines across the country.

It was a beautiful thing to see because the country was finally—finally—seeing the real Daly. A drunk, spoiled brat who police described as "uncooperative."

But this is the real kicker and why Daly is a top 10 jerk: Daly is as much of an excuse-maker as he is a drunk. The reason police were called was because Daly was so out of it, his friends were concerned. He was on the ground looking dazed with his eyes wide open.

Daly's explanation is priceless and will go down in history as one of the great excuses of all time. The reason he looked so drunk, the reason he looked practically dead on the ground, not moving, his eyes wide open, is because he sometimes sleeps with his eyes open.

Please digest that for a moment. He sleeps with his eyes open—that was his excuse. John Daly: drunken vampire. Does Daly only drink after the sun goes down, as well?

"If I had seen someone like that," Daly told the Associated Press, referring to him being drunk and out of it, "I probably would have done the same thing. They were only trying to protect me."

"The thing I want people to know is when I called my girlfriend at 11:30 PM, I was going back to the bus to go sleep," Daly told the AP, elaborating on his inebriation. "I'm not going to say I wasn't drunk. I did have a few drinks. I said to them, 'I'm tired, I'm drunk, and I'm going to bed.'"

He had a few drinks.

When's the last time you had a "few drinks" and ended up having friends so concerned that they called 911?

"The bus driver called 911 because my eyes were open," Daly said, according to the AP. "I said, 'What's going on?' He said, 'We thought you were dead.' Anybody who knows me…when I'm tired, I sleep with my eyes open. They know it takes awhile to wake me up."

Well, hell. Of course. Why wouldn't anyone know that when Daly gets tired, *he sleeps with his eyes open*?

How stupid of us.

"The picture looks like I'm drunk," the AP quotes Daly as saying. "I wasn't drunk when they took the picture. The picture people are seeing is me half-asleep."

Half-asleep, drunk. Drunk, half-asleep. What's the difference? There may not be a bigger waste of human life than one John "Eyes Wide Shut" Daly.

We could detail all of Daly's transgressions, but we don't want to overdo it. You know how horrific he's been both as a golfer and a human being. It seems the only person who doesn't get it is Daly. He's surrounded himself with sycophants and small legal minds (very small) that tell him he's fine, and Daly isn't the kind of person who takes a great deal of responsibility.

This point must be emphasized. Not only does Daly need to look in the mirror, but his excuse-makers (as small in number as they're getting) also need to take a hard look at themselves. Because one day Daly's drinking is going to lead to something other than Daly ending up in an embarrassing jumpsuit telling lies about sleeping with his eyes open. Something much more serious will happen, probably to someone else, as a result of Daly's incompetence and inebriation.

Daly Jokes

Before we move on, three quick Daly jokes that were told to us by a PGA Tour golfer. We've been informed that some people on the tour constantly make fun of Daly's weight and ineptitude.

1 – The reason Daly is now one of the worst golfers on the planet is because when he gets on a roll, he stops to eat it.

2 – Normally when you see a face like Daly's, there's a bag of oats in front of it.

3 – When Daly has sex, it's like two pancakes fighting over butter.

Daly Sued Me

Before we move on, part two.

Daly sued me for defamation of character several years ago when I wrote a column about him that in my opinion (and the opinion of others) was accurate and truthful. To this day, I don't know why he sued, except for the fact that maybe the column was too accurate and hit too close to home. So we wanted to get that out of the way. We're writing a book about the experience, in fact, with the cornerstone of the book being Daly's PGA Tour file. It's a file you won't believe once it becomes public (and we're going to make it public—it might even be public by the time you read this).

If you think I'm ripping Daly because of that, you couldn't be more wrong. I've long thought Daly symbolized the gross double standard in professional sports. Daly's been excused by the media, the lazy PGA Tour, and advertisers for being a waste and drunk while crucifying athletes with similar backgrounds like Pacman Jones and Allen Iverson. Until recently, some of the golf media—emphasis on some—have ignored Daly's uselessness and downfall fearing his popularity with the fans.

Incredibly, Daly has been such a joke, such a waste, that even some of his strongest backers in the press have now abandoned him. So have many in the golf world. Who can forget the excellent quote from swing coach Butch Harmon. Daly had hired Harmon to help his game, but Harmon lasted just one week before quitting. The event that put Harmon over the top was when Daly spent a rain delay in a Hooters tent (Hooters must be very proud of their top pitchman) and then returned to action with Tampa Bay Buccaneers coach Jon Gruden as his caddie. It was yet another show of unprofessional behavior from Daly.

Harmon was furious and said, "my whole goal for [Daly] was he's got to show me golf is the most important thing in his life. And the most important thing in his life is getting drunk."

It was a great quote. Daly did as he often does. Instead of looking in the mirror at his own behavior, Daly blamed Harmon.

Harmon responded with another outstanding quote, "John keeps denying that all of his problems are his own doing. He needs to take responsibility for his actions."

It really doesn't get more accurate than that.

Tim Donaghy

D avid Stern is one of my favorite people in the world. He's smart, proactive, and talented. Each time I've spoken to Stern, he's also always upbeat. He's a strong defender of his league. The only time I've ever seen Stern look, well, sad was when he met the press to discuss the Tim Donaghy scandal.

"I have been involved with refereeing and obviously been involved with the NBA for 40 years in some shape or form," Stern said that day to the media. "I can tell you that this is the most serious situation and worst situation that I have ever experienced either as a fan of the NBA, a lawyer for the NBA, or a commissioner of the NBA. And we take our obligation to our fans in this matter very, very seriously, and I can stand here today and pledge that we will do every look-back possible to analyze our processes and seek the best advice possible to see if there are changes that should be made and procedures that should be implemented to continue to assure fans that we are doing the best we possibly can. It's small consolation to me, but, you know, doing the best you can doesn't always mean that criminal activity by a determined person can be prevented. All you can do in many cases is deal with it as harshly as you can when you determine it and hope that that, in addition to all of your other processes and procedures, acts as a deterrent."

Stern handled the situation well, and he was right. What Donaghy did was expose just how easy it is for a game official to cheat and drastically alter the outcome of games. Donaghy

Former NBA official Tim Donaghy talks with another official during a timeout during a Washington Wizards–New Jersey Nets basketball game on Tuesday, April 10, 2007, in Washington.

was the cause of nightmares not just in the NBA but among all leagues and fans.

"Now that it has happened," wrote then *Boston Globe* columnist Jackie MacMullan, "you realize with frightening clarity how feasible—and how damning—it would be for referees, umpires, or linesmen to be corrupt, and how lucky the four major professional sports leagues in our country have been not to have confronted this issue before."

We will never know exactly how much damage Donaghy did. Our feeling at Jerk Central is that Donaghy was like a spy working for the old Soviet Union. The amount of actual intelligence the spy sent to his bosses before being caught is difficult to determine. Just how many games Donaghy bet on and outcomes he affected Donaghy has likely kept to himself and will never reveal, no matter what the NBA or FBI says.

We also won't know about the accuracy of Stern's contention that Donaghy was a rogue official. It might be true, but it's also possible Donaghy wasn't alone. That's why his case is so frightening. All this time later, there are still a great many unknowns.

In August 2007, Donaghy pled guilty to two counts related to his gambling on games, specifically pleading to wire fraud and transmitting wagering information through interstate commerce. He was sentenced to 15 months in prison.

"Every news account begins with the words 'disgraced referee,'" his attorney said at the time. "He will live with that the rest of his life."

Donaghy will have to live with his actions forever. And so will the rest of us.

Michael Vick

There are a handful of moments when you remember exactly where you were. When Michael Vick was sentenced to prison in 2007, I watched the news on television from my home. There was no real feeling of sympathy. Vick, I thought, got what he deserved.

Part of how you felt about Vick depended on your relationship with dogs. If you had a dog, you despised Vick. If you didn't,

Michael Vick leaves federal court after pleading guilty to a dogfighting charge in Richmond, Virginia, on August 27, 2007. (AP Photo)

you still likely thought what Vick did was wrong, but his fighting of dogs didn't affect you as personally. Polls also showed race was a factor. Blacks, it seemed, particularly in Atlanta, didn't think Vick's crimes were as severe as whites did.

Indeed, there was an interesting cultural phenomenon at work in Vick's case. White friends in Atlanta were befuddled by how some blacks could ever support someone who was so cruel to animals. Blacks cited hypocrisy. Why is it okay, I was asked by blacks, to eat animals but a federal crime to fight them? I'm African American with American Indian ancestry whose mother is African American with Irish ancestry. I grew up in one of the first planned communities in the world that emphasized multiculturalism and am married to a white woman. I traverse easily through many different worlds (though I'm firmly rooted in the African American one). To me this was a simple matter, and as usual, race was making the Vick case more complicated than it needed to be. To me, Vick was an embarrassment to our people—black people, a cruel human being, and an Uncle Tom who blew a great opportunity to be the hero of a city that sometimes is in desperate need of one.

Atlanta is one of my favorite places mainly because it reminds me of my birthplace in Washington. Both are full of beautiful people, and both have seen their share of great pain. Vick was a unifying force in Atlanta. He could've owned Atlanta the way Babe Ruth once owned New York. That's not an exaggeration. He was at one point that beloved and then, just as suddenly, he became an arrogant ass.

One of the best PR men in all of sports is Reggie Roberts, who works for the Atlanta Falcons. He set me up once with a brief Vick interview and to put it mildly, Vick was a jerk. Roberts told me, "He just needs to grow up." And that was before the dog fiasco.

Yes, Vick did need to grow up, but before he could, a number of animals needlessly suffered. I actually understand the point that the difference between cutting off a chicken's head and eating it or killing a horse after its usefulness on a racetrack has expired—and dog fighting—is not as great as some state, and there's the definite appearance of hypocrisy. What Vick did was nevertheless indefensible. According to the government indictment, eight dogs were put to death at a home owned by Vick. The indictment stated that the dogs were killed "by hanging, drowning and/or slamming at least one dog's body to the ground." Another dog that lost in a fight was killed when it was wet with water and electrocuted.

He was the catalyst for a dog-fighting ring, either killed or supervised the killing of some underperforming dogs, and was suspended indefinitely by the NFL. "Your admitted conduct was not only illegal, but also cruel and reprehensible," wrote NFL Commissioner Roger Goodell to Vick. "Your team, the NFL, and NFL fans have all been hurt by your actions...Your plea agreement and the plea agreements of your co-defendants also demonstrate your significant involvement in illegal gambling. Even if you personally did not place bets, as you contend, your actions in funding the betting and your association with illegal gambling both violate the terms of your NFL Player Contract and expose you to corrupting influences in derogation of one of the most fundamental responsibilities of an NFL player."

Vick was sentenced to 23 months in prison in Leavenworth, Kansas, following pleading guilty to running a dog-fighting operation. He's scheduled to be released in July 2009.

Will Vick play football in the NFL again? Of course he will. Some team will remember that incredible speed and athleticism and play Vick at wide receiver or running back. It will happen because NFL teams would hire a mass-murderer if he could run a 4.4-second 40-yard dash.

When Vick gets out, just keep the pit bulls away from him. In fact, make sure the only pets Vick has are goldfish. You can't train goldfish to fight, can you?

Roger Clemens

In February 2008, Roger Clemens sat just a short few feet away from me at a Congressional committee hearing in Washington. Just a few feet from him was the man who'd accused Clemens of using steroids, Brian McNamee. It was a fascinating moment in sports history that won't soon be forgotten.

Roger Clemens is sworn in on Capitol Hill in Washington D.C., on Wednesday, February 13, 2008, prior to testifying before the House Oversight and Government Reform committee hearing on drug use in baseball. (AP Photo/ Pablo Martinez Monsivais, Susan Walsh)

I was blogging about Clemens' testimony but could hardly focus on anyone or anything but Clemens who swore under oath that he never took steroids. It was reminiscent of when Rafael Palmeiro waved his little finger before a Congressional panel and said he never utilized performance-enhancing drugs either. Palmeiro lied, and many people watching the ceremony on live television both in the room and around the country probably felt the same way about Clemens.

McNamee utterly destroyed Clemens. It was obvious who had more credibility as Clemens was dissected on many different fronts. Clemens claimed—under oath—that he never spoke about performance-enhancing drugs with McNamee and that McNamee injected Clemens with only vitamins and lidocaine. Where Clemens was truly caught in a lie was that former Yankees teammate Andy Pettite testified that Clemens had informed him

McNamee had injected Clemens with HGH. It led most rational people to ask the question: why would Pettite not only lie about his best friend Clemens but risk being persecuted for perjury in doing so?

Congressional officials definitely didn't believe Clemens. "Roger Clemens failed to convince Congress he was telling the truth," wrote the Associated Press in 2008.

"We are not in a position to reach a definitive judgment as to whether Mr. Clemens lied to the committee," Congressional leaders Henry Waxman and Tom Davis wrote to Attorney General Michael Mukasey. "Our only conclusion is that significant questions have been raised about Mr. Clemens' truthfulness."

No kidding.

Congress asked for a Justice Department investigation, and Clemens was officially in deep trouble.

Now, this is the point where—though it would've been late—Clemens should have come clean. "I'm sorry," he could have said at this point. "I was a fart-face. I lied because I wanted to protect my legacy. I accept whatever punishment you give me. If you want to throw me in fart face prison, so be it. I'm going to be an adult and take my punishment like an adult." Well, maybe not the fart face part, but you get the point.

That's what Marion Jones did. She lied so much her nose had grown to the size of Arizona, but she finally dropped the facade and admitted the truth. Clemens? Not only did Clemens refuse to come clean, he actually sued McNamee for defamation. Clemens was putting his character at stake, which was a risky proposition particularly considering the news that emerged about Clemens in April 2008. The *New York Daily News* reported that Clemens, despite being a long-married father of four children, had multiple affairs.

"It never should have been filed to begin with," law professor Peter Keane told the *Daily News*, referring to Clemens' defamation suit. "Since he is claiming his reputation has been damaged, it is relevant to the lawsuit to ask what kind of reputation does he have. You can't compartmentalize your reputation...It is not about individual ingredients. It is one big, bubbling stew pot." Keane added that the former Yankees pitcher had a nearly impossible mission in winning the suit and that was before news of Clemens' alleged infidelity. "Everything he has done is geared to self-destruction," Keane said. "It's like watching a lemming heading for the waves."

Clemens at times seemed to be reaching for anything to discredit McNamee. When Clemens did an interview on *60 Minutes,* he said McNamee lied to cover up the fact that McNamee—according to Clemens—was trafficking steroids. There was no proof that that was true.

McNamee is no prince, but Clemens is far worse. McNamee seemed to come to terms with who he was and what he did. Clemens has yet to do that. Clemens still lives in a fantasy world where he never used performance-enhancing drugs. Unfortunately for Clemens, that world has a population of just a handful of people. Members of Congress didn't believe him and most people don't either. Actually, maybe that fantasy world inhabited by Clemens has a population of just one.

Rae Carruth

Can a murderer be a jerk?
Does naming a murderer as a simple jerk cheapen the horrific act the murderer committed? These are fair questions,

Former Carolina Panthers receiver Rae Carruth, center, smiles as he talks with his attorney David Rudolf, left, on Wednesday, November 29, 2000, before the continuation of his murder trial in Charlotte, North Carolina. (AP Photo/Jeff Siner/Charlotte Observer)

and I'm not even certain I have the answers. I've contemplated this issue both in my (convoluted) head and in writings online. I've decided there is no better response to a murderer than to mock the murderer. Besides, it's impossible to compose a book of historic jerk athletes without having Rae Carruth and O.J. Simpson on it. That would be like putting on *Hamlet* without Hamlet or *Star Trek* without Nichelle Nichols wearing one of those short skirts.

Carruth should be released from a North Carolina prison in 2018. If there were justice in this world, someone would shoot Carruth on his drive home from jail. We're not asking anyone to do that. Let's be clear. We're not. We're not asking anyone to do it. Is that clear enough? But it sure would be nice if it occurred.

Then Carruth would know what it was like to suffer the fate of his girlfriend, whom Carruth conspired to kill while she was pregnant. She was gunned down in her car while pregnant with Carruth's twins.

What's interesting about Carruth's case is that you wonder how much being a professional athlete emboldened him to plot this macabre and disgraceful conspiracy. If he were just a bricklayer, would Carruth have done this? Did athlete arrogance play a critical part? Is that even a proper question to pose?

If there is one commonality among these jerks, it is arrogance. Many of them feel that rules and societal mores don't apply to them. The vast majority of them don't become murderers, of course, but if there was a potential poster child for this type of arrogance, it's Carruth. When Cherica Adams became pregnant with Carruth's child, something snapped in Carruth. He decided neither Adams or his own children should live. What would make someone reach that conclusion is puzzling—to say the least—to most people.

Despite being shot four times, Adams was still able to call emergency services. She died days later, but one of the children survived and is alive today (unfortunately, he was born with cerebral palsy). Carruth fled and was found hiding in a trunk like a coward. He was convicted of conspiracy to commit murder, shooting into an occupied vehicle, and killing an unborn child. Adams was eight months pregnant at the time of the shootings.

"I would like to hear why he committed the act," Adams' father, Jeffrey Moonie, told the media after the trial. "I'm still surprised he has not shown any reaction so far."

It's the ultimate question: why would anyone kill a pregnant woman? It's a question Carruth has yet to answer and probably never will.

Good Guys

And before you get all depressed over being surrounded by a world full of jerks, here are five really, really good guys:

5. **Ernie Accorsi** – Former NFL general manager and now special assistant to the NFL. A football historian and friendly soul.

4. **Mike Silver** – Yahoo! Sports (never forget the exclamation point) writer who is classy and funny both in person and in his column.

3. **President Obama** – Pushing for a college football playoff.

2. **Mark Messier** – Tough guy on the ice, nice guy off of it.

1. **Tim Tebow** – One of the nicest and most genuine guys we've ever seen in college sports.

O.J. Simpson

Nothing better has ever been written about Orenthal James Simpson than the following column by the late Ralph Wiley, one of the great sports journalists of the twentieth century, for ESPN.com. It's so good we're running a portion of it here. Please read Wiley's words carefully. This portion is lengthy but it's vital, and trust us—it's worth it. He begins by mentioning an HBO documentary on Simpson:

> "HBO's latest sports documentary says it's an examination of race relations throughout O.J. Simpson's

O.J. Simpson appears in court during his sentencing hearing at the Clark County Regional Justice Center in Las Vegas, Nevada, on Friday, December 5, 2008. (AP Photo/ Isaac Brekken)

life, a 'Study in Black and White.' Actually, it's a study in white. It toes a media party line that white is right and black is base. There are knowing lines within the documentary, but they are blunted by an overall naiveté.

"The documentary's most honest trait is its brevity— some 49 minutes in length. Why? Because, when you get down to it, at the center of O.J. Simpson, there was nothing there. Nada. If ever there was not only a colorless but soulless man, it was him.

"Yet the documentary starts off with him saying, 'I'm a black guy, always been a black guy, never been nothing but a black guy.'

"This is disingenuous. O.J. tried and almost succeeded at being everything but a black guy—and, more important, his own guy.

"He fooled himself. He fooled white people. But he didn't fool very many black people. Not the ones who knew him well, anyway.

"O.J. Simpson could be and often was base. Jim Brown knew it. Harry Edwards knew it. His first wife Marguerite (whom he stole from his black 'best friend,' Al Cowlings) knew it. I learned it. To people like us, there was no arguing it.

"But not to white people, especially the captains of industry Juice performed for. His off-screen antics made Stepin Fetchit look like Frederick Douglass.

"No, we were all the difficult ones. We were the ones who didn't understand how to be, how to go along to get along. If a black man is grinning all the time, being obsequious, that is seen as some kind of righteousness; meanwhile, those seeing it that way never seem to understand that no person can live a life of mental duplicity for very long without something beginning to slip upstairs.

"In the doc, former sociology professor at Cal-Berkeley Harry Edwards says Simpson, 'bought the hype,' because it brought him a rich lifestyle. Juice played long before the big multi-million dollar contracts. Yet he lived like a prince. Traits like self-respect, personal responsibility, personal excellence, not just on a playing field, and community responsibility and plain common sense have nothing to do with fooling people.

"O.J. fooled a lot of people.

"Few of them were black."

• • •

Simpson fooled a lot of people, white and black. Hell, of all races. He fooled men and women, business tycoons, the media, coaches, and the like. He was an equal-opportunity fooler.

I'm proud to say, bragging really, that I was one of the few who knew Simpson was a gold-plated phony. No, it's true. I met Simpson many years ago, before the murders in Los Angeles, before the recent news of Simpson going to prison for robbery when he got off for murder. He was still working as a television analyst, and I'd just gotten into journalism. We met at Giants Stadium after I saw Simpson and approached him. I introduced myself. He was friendly and gregarious and then he said, "I've been reading your stuff for years." I hadn't been in the business for years.

Well, hell, I thought. He was just trying to be nice and misspoke. Not a big deal. Then he did something really odd and, truthfully, infuriating. Remember, we'd just met. I'm paraphrasing, but Simpson basically said, "Just one piece of advice. Don't become one of those radical brothers in sports writing."

I asked Simpson what he meant by "radical."

This is almost an exact quote. "Don't be talking race this and race that," he said.

"That…that's your advice?" I thought. He was basically saying—don't rustle any feathers. Or, more succinctly, Simpson was telling me to blend in.

The way he did.

• • •

But there's a tremendous leap from being publicly passive to becoming a murderer. Simpson was held liable in civil court for the deaths of his ex-wife Nicole Brown Simpson and Ronald Goldman. Simpson was ordered to pay $33.5 million and has yet to pay almost any of the judgment.

What happened to Simpson? He admittedly never took a substantive stance. He was never Jim Brown or Jackie Robinson or Ali. In fairness, not many athletes are. It's dangerous to take any kind of serious social position because of the extensive public repercussions. When an athlete has strong opinions, marketing opportunities dry up and fans shy away.

Simpson's jerk/murder/turd credentials are top of the line. Well, he killed two people. That right there is douchebag material. And if there is anyone who still doubts that he did it, well, you're a fool. You also believe the moon landing was faked. You should be in a mental institution. Of course he did it.

Instead of crawling into a hole, Simpson went golfing while looking for the real killer. To make matters worse, he wrote a book called *If I Did It.* In the book, Simpson plays the hypothetical role speculating how the murders would've occurred if he had committed them. Simpson demonstrated that not only didn't he have remorse over the murders, he was willing to profit from them and almost taunt the legal system that rewarded him with a non-guilty verdict in the murder trial.

Back to the main question: what happened to Simpson? How did he develop into a killer? My theory? My amateur psychologist theory? It goes back to Wiley's quote—he fooled a lot of people. I think Simpson likely always held pathological and violent tendencies. He just hid them. In the murder trial, it was clear he had a violent temper, and when he was sent to prison in 2008 for robbery, again, we saw that temper. He fooled a lot of people until he lost his temper in the most violent of ways by killing two people.

He fooled a lot of people over and over and over again for much of his life.

He's unlike other jerks who were simple buffoons, excuse-makers, and clowns (see Daly, John). He was just a deeply awful human being. Even Carruth didn't write a book. (Though Daly is considering writing a book called *If I Ate It...The Sad Tale of that Last Donut.*)

• • •

Since Wiley probably penned the best thing ever written about Simpson, it's Wiley who gets the last word. "I met Juice later," Wiley wrote. "We worked on the same set of NBC's NFL Live in 1989. That's where I got to know him. You don't need all the gory details here. He played a little game for the bosses, involving stories of sexual exploits, titty bars, and what-not. Part of his role was to belittle...if not outright destroy...any other so-called black person in the vicinity. Even back then, Jim Brown told me, 'You better watch him, Wiley. That m-----f-----'s dangerous.'

"The HBO doc purports that O.J. opened all these doors in TV and cinema. No, he didn't. If it had been up to Juice, nobody would have gone through those doors except him. Jim Brown, Woody Strode, and Michael Warren opened doors. Jim had already been a movie star. His filmography comes up short when compared to Denzel Washington's, but with *The Dirty Dozen, Ice Station Zebra,* and *100 Rifles* alone, he did way more than Juice.

"Juice's great role was bamboozling white folks. And himself.

"He began to 'buy the hype,' as Harry Edwards said, meaning he thought he had a divine right, divine privileges. Once, one of his producers told me he said he thought he was the son of God. I'd tried to throw Juice a rope. 'Well, we're all children of God,' I said. 'No,' said the producer. 'He said the son of God.'"

I believe the story. It's not difficult to see how Simpson thought he was Jesus Christ.

He fooled a lot of people.

Over and over and over again.

Acknowledgments

Now I know what it was like to write the Constitution. Except *Jerks* was far tougher to compose. In terms of difficulty to compose, there's *Jerks*, the Bill of Rights, the Gettysburg Address, and the "I Have a Dream" speech. In that order, to be exact.

First, I'd like to thank the jerks themselves. Without you, sexy jerks, this book would not have been possible. Please, keep getting your jerk on. I'd like to do a sequel.

I'd also like to thank Mark Swanson, my boss at CBSSports. com, one of the best in the business, and as always, my trustworthy agent John Monteleone.

Most of all, I'd like to thank Triumph Books for giving me the opportunity to put my asinine thoughts in print. My development editor at Triumph, Adam Motin, is patient and smart, and he needed lots of both to deal with me. Associate Editor Karen O'Brien was a tremendous asset and the opposite of jerky.

And a Few Other Jerks for Your Amusement...

Several who just missed the Jerkitude 100:

Jeremy Foley—Arrogant athletic director at the University of Florida who likes to verbally berate journalists.

Stadium songs—Annoying.

Rogers Hornsby—An alleged member of the Ku Klux Klan and compulsive gambler.

Steve Howe—Suspended seven times for drug use.

Rick Neuheisel—Jackass.

The Portland Jail Blazers—Before the Bengals, there were the Jail Blazers.

Floyd Landis—Refuses to admit he cheated.

Maurice Clarett—Knucklehead.

Jim Brown—Hate making this mention, but Brown's had an issue with his temper and women.

The site Every Day Should Be Saturday—Garbage. Horribly written putrid garbage.

John Stockton—Notorious for dirty play.

Any idiot who starts fire (insert name of coach or journalists here). com.

Ricky Williams—Almost smoked his career away.

Ryan Leaf—Notorious bust.

Bill Laimbeer—See Stockton, John.

And finally...Charlie Weis. We end with this portion of an outstanding column on Weis by *Chicago Tribune* writer Teddy Greenstein. It begins: "The guy who once boasted he 'could get hoodlums and thugs and win tomorrow' strolled into Jeannette High School in the spring of 2007 to recruit superstar quarterback Terrelle Pryor. Jeannette coach Ray Reitz knew a bit about Charlie Weis and his reputation. Still, he was stunned by what he describes as a level of conceit he never had seen from the dozens of college coaches he had visited with over the years. Weis certainly made a lasting impression.

"'Arrogant as hell,' Reitz said.

"When Reitz told Weis that Pryor might attend a USC quarterbacks camp, he remembers Weis replying, 'Why send him there? If he's with me for one day he'll be good, two days he'll be great, and three days he'll be incredible.' Later, unprompted, Weis asked the Jeannette coaches if they wanted to take a picture of his Super Bowl ring. 'I did it, just to be polite, and then gave [the picture] to one of the kids,' Reitz recalled."

We thought that was a great way to end a book about jerks.

About the Author

Kelly Whiteside

Michael Freeman is a national columnist for CBSSports. com. He has previously worked for the *Florida Times-Union*, *New York Times*, *Washington Post*, *Boston Globe*, and *Dallas Morning News*. Freeman is the author of three other books, including *Bloody Sundays*, which was a *New York Times* notable book. He is also the author of *Jim Brown: The Fierce Life of An American Hero*, a finalist for best biography in the 2007 NAACP Image Awards. In 2006, he became one of only a handful of writers ever to win three Associated Press Sports Editors top-ten writing awards in one year. He lives with his wife and dog in New Jersey. And, yes, sometimes he acts like a jerk.